I0502426

Famous

Painters

In Art History

A Coloring & Guide Book

Written & Illustrated by Davina Rush

Other Titles By Davina Rush

Creatures of Greek Mythology
Creatures of Classic Horror
Alice in Wonderland
Haunted Dolls

Famous Painters in Art History

with more to come!

Keep up to date on the latest publications
www.DavinaRush.Com
Facebook.com/DavinaRush

Copyright ©December 2016 by Davina Rush

ISBN-13: 978-1541112247

ISBN-10: 1541112245

All rights reserved. This book and all material within is protected by copyright and may not be reproduced in whole or in part or in any other form or format without written permission directly from the author or from her power of attorney.

This publication is intended to provide general information and entertainment. The author has researched the material contained within this book but does not claim to be an expert in any of the subject matter presented here. All coloring page illustrations within this book are creative interpretations of the original art and in no way, claim to be exact replicas of the original paintings that they represent. For more information on the presented work and corresponding artists, it is recommended that you do further research online and/or at your local library.

This book is dedicated to...

the very special people who have actively encouraged me in my many creative endeavors. Every artist in the world shines in their own unique way, but we are made far greater by the light that shines in the eyes of those who believe in us, those special people who kindle our creative fire by lending a little spark of their own-- the many muses embodied in the friends and family that surround us every day, pushing us forward. You are all greatly appreciated and loved!

For Grandma

Content

Foreword

Learning about art history doesn't have to be all textbooks, essays and tests; it can also be great hands-on fun! In this book, you will learn interesting and educational facts about *The Famous Painters in Art History* AND you'll get to enjoy coloring an illustrated rendering of each one of the artist's paintings. Challenge yourself to color like the masters by referencing the colored originals, available online, using the titles and dates that have been provided for each painting. Or create your own version of these masterpieces, changing colors and textures as you please.

Note

Each painting is presented with its title listed above the illustration. With this information, you can search for the original images online, so that you may reference them for color and technique, textures and shading. You may choose to color the images in accordance with the original, or you might choose to create your own unique color palette.

In addition, I would like to say that I have included information about each artist, but these fun facts are barely even the tip of the iceberg for these monumental historical figures. I strongly recommend further reading on each of these artists, as their stories have so many interesting twists and turns, details that I could not modestly fit into this book without turning it into a huge textbook. I have also included, with a few of the biographies, a movie recommendation portraying the artist and a facet of their lifetime; movies that I, personally, have greatly enjoyed.

Famous

Painters

In Art History

A Coloring & Guide Book

Written & Illustrated by Davina Rush

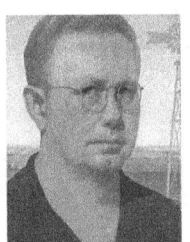

Grant Wood
(February 13, 1891 – February 12, 1942)

Grant DeVolson Wood was born on February 13, 1891, on a farm near Anamosa, Iowa. His parents were Francis Maryville Wood and Hattie Weaver, both farmers. Grant had three siblings; Frank, Jack and Nan. His sister, Nan Wood Graham, is well known as the female model in his painting, *American Gothic.*

Around the age of 10, Grant's father died unexpectedly, forcing his mother to sell the farm and move the family to Cedar Rapids, Iowa. Soon after, Wood began an apprenticeship in metal working. Later, after graduating high school, he enrolled in the Handicraft Guild of Minneapolis. In 1913 he attended the School of the Art Institute of Chicago. Around 1922 and over the span of around 6 years, Wood made four trips to Europe, where he studied many styles of painting. He took a special interest in Impressionism. In 1932 Wood helped in founding the Stone City Art Colony; an establishment focused on helping artists through the Great Depression. From 1934 to 1941 he taught at the University of Iowa's School of Art.

As a painter, Wood was best known for his depictions of the rural farm life that had surrounded him as a child, his best-known piece being *American Gothic.* These works are associated with the American art movement of *Regionalism;* a style and theme in painting that conveys a sense of romantic nationalism through illustrations of everyday life. While Wood is best known for his paintings, he also worked in a variety of other media; charcoal, lithography, ceramics, metal, ink and wood.

In 1935, Grant Wood married Sara Sherman Maxon, a former opera singer. The relationship, unfortunately, did not last and ended with a divorce in 1938. The couple had no children together.

On February 12, 1942, only one day before his 51st birthday, Grant DeVolson Wood died at the university hospital, succumbing to pancreatic cancer. His estate went to his sister, Nan Wood Graham. The estate later became the property of the Figge Art Museum in Davenport. Wood was later deemed the patron artist of Cedar Rapids, with his childhood schoolhouse depicted on the 2004 Iowa State Quarter.

American Gothic, Wood's best known piece of work, depicts a farmer and his spinster daughter (not his wife, as commonly thought). These characters were modeled by the artist's sister, Nan and by his dentist, Dr. Byron McKeeby.

American Gothic (1930) by Grant Wood

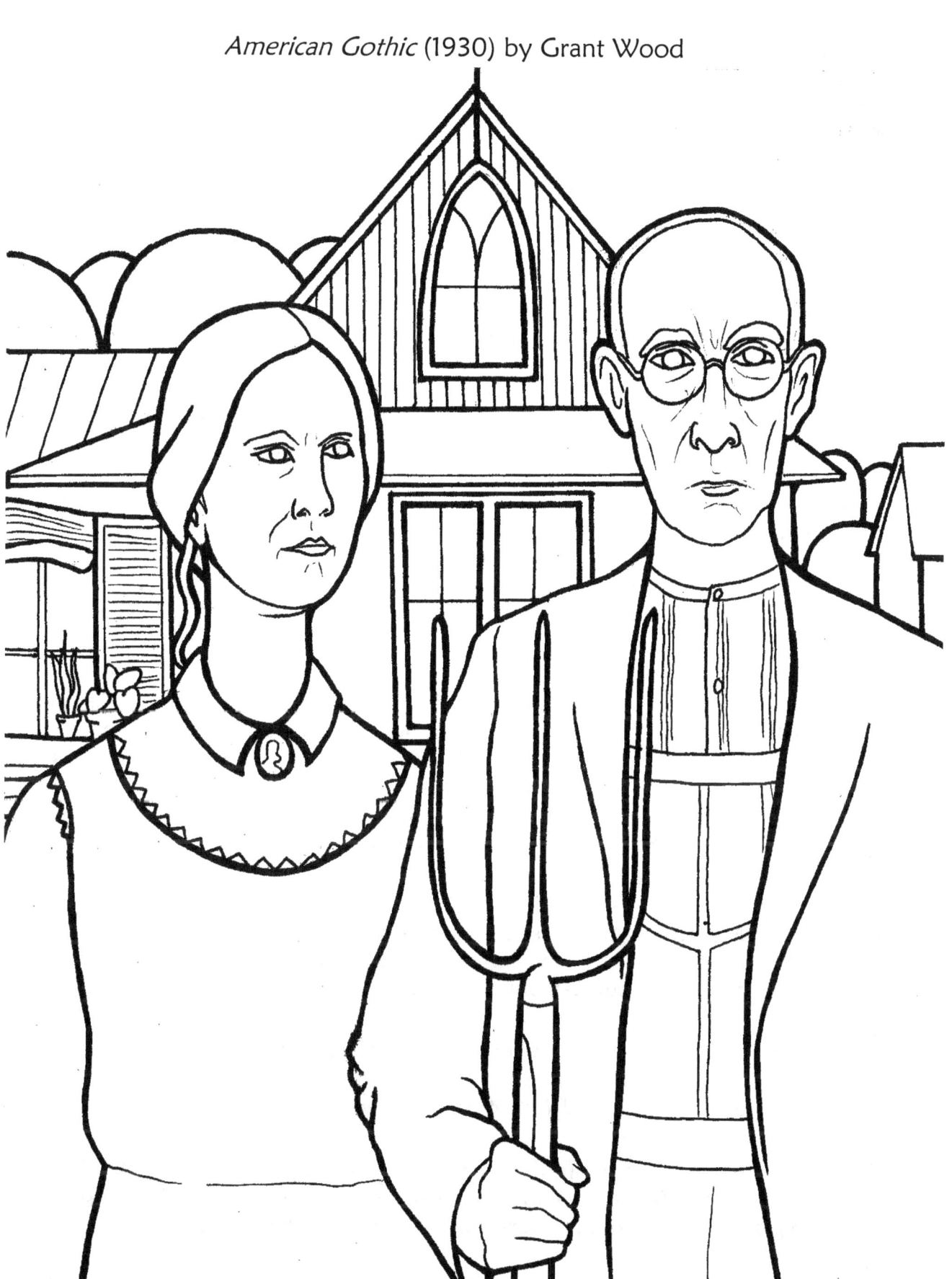

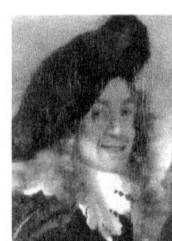

Johannes Vermeer
(Oct 31, 1632 - Dec 15, 1675)

Johannes Vermeer was born in Delft, of the Dutch Republic and baptized on the 31ˢᵗ of October in 1632. His father, Reijnier Janszoon Vermeer, was a middle-class silk worker; his mother was Digna Baltus. Johannes had one older sister, Geertruy.

It is not known for sure where or to whom Vermeer was apprenticed with as a painter, it has been suggested that perhaps he was self-taught. Vermeer's father was an art dealer and this is possibly where Vermeer's passion for painting began. After his father's death, in 1652, Vermeer assumed operation of the family's business and was himself an art dealer. On December 29ᵗʰ, 1653, Vermeer joined the Guild of Saint Luke; a guild of artists, named for the Evangelist, Luke, the patron saint of artists. In 1662, Vermeer was chosen as head of the guild and was later reelected multiple times. In 1657, he acquired the patronage of Pieter van Ruijven, a well-known, local art collector that would commission many pieces from the artist,

Vermeer was known to work slowly, producing maybe 3 paintings in one year's time; finishing only around 34 masterpieces in his lifetime. He took great care in his work, paying close attention to detail and the mastery of light and color. He painted mostly domestic scenes that were set up inside of his own home, in Delft. One trademark aspect of Vermeer's meticulous painting technique was his choice of pigments. He is best known for his favored use of the very expensive ultramarine blue, lead-tin-yellow, madder lake, vermilion, ochres, bone black and azurite.

On April 5ᵗʰ, 1653, Johannes Reijniersz Vermeer was wed to Catharina Bolenes; a young Catholic girl. They had 10 children together: Maria, Elisabeth, Cornelia, Aleydis, Beatrix, Johannes, Gertruyd, Franciscus, Catharina, and Ignatius.

Vermeer passed away on December 15, 1675, after a brief illness. He is buried in the Protestant Old Church (Oude Kerk), in Delft. His wife, Catharina, believed that it was the stress and pressures of their financial situation that ultimately killed him.

Vermeer was a respected artist in Delft, but he was almost unknown outside of his hometown during his lifetime. He was rediscovered in the 19ᵗʰ century and is now known as one of the greatest painters of the Dutch Golden Age; the Master of Light.

Johannes Vermeer is wonderfully portrayed in the visually stunning 2003 film, *Girl with a Pearl Earring;* starring Scarlett Johansson and Colin Firth.

The Milk Maid/ The Kitchen Maid (c. 1657-58) by Johannes Vermeer

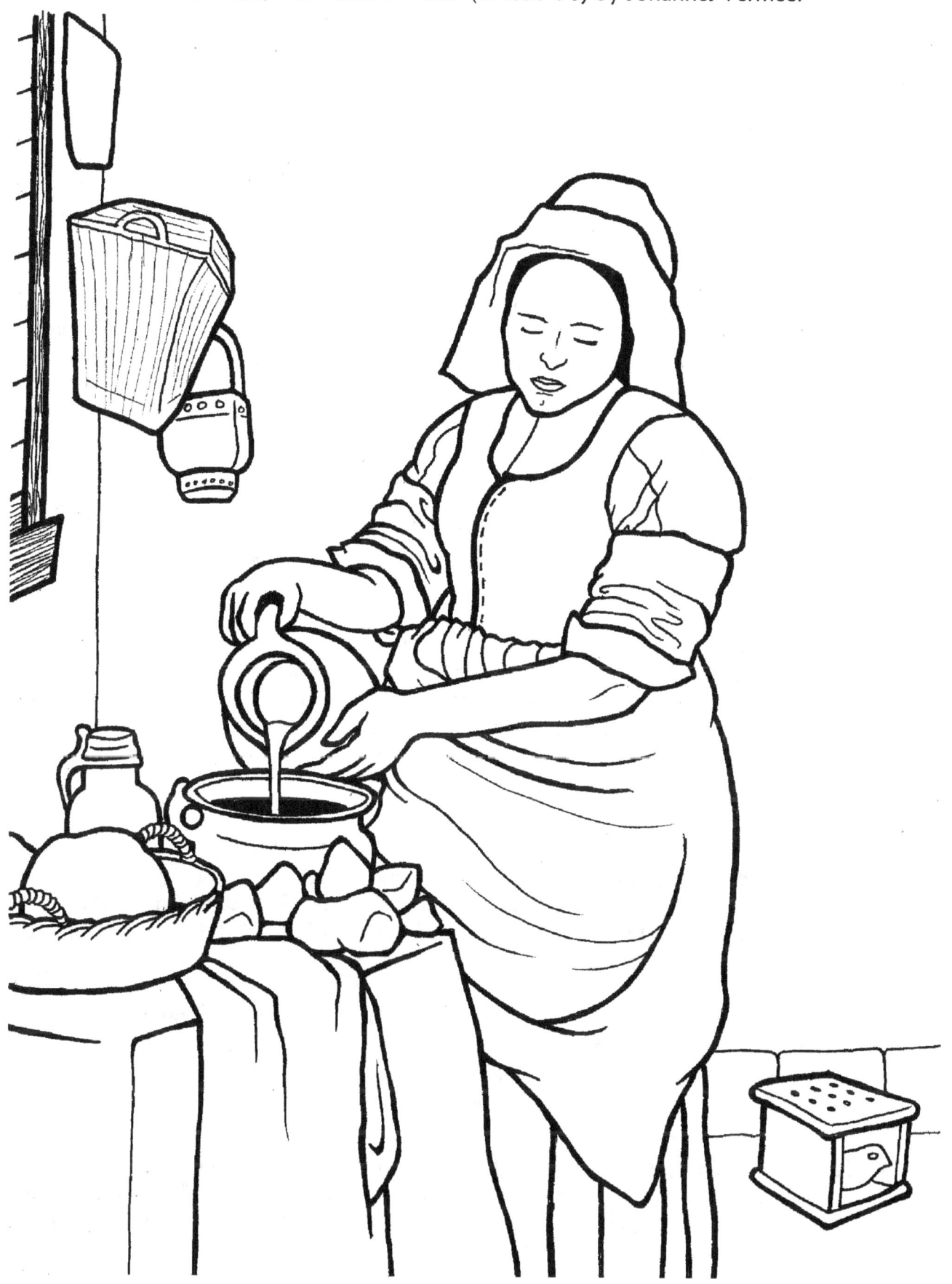

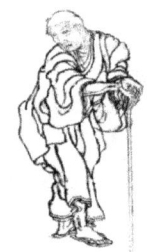

Katsushika Hokusai
(October 1760 – May 10, 1849)

Katsushika Hokusai's exact date of birth is uncertain, but is said to have been sometime in October of 1760, in Edo (now Tokyo), Japan. His father, Nakajima Ise, was a mirror-maker for the shogun. Hokusai was never named as an heir to his father, so it is believed that his mother may have been a concubine.

Hokusai began painting when he was around six years of age, possibly learning the skill from his father. When he was around 12 years old, his father sent him to work in a bookshop. At 14, Hokusai was taken on as an apprentice by a wood-carver, where he worked and studied for 4 years. When he was 18, he was accepted into the studio of Katsukawa Shunshō, an artist who worked with ukiyo-e, a style of wood block printing and painting that Hokusai would someday be best-known for.

Hokusai had at least thirty names that he was known by throughout his lifetime. Using multiple names was not uncommon among the Japanese artists of his time; changing their signature as their art style evolved over the years. Hokusai's name changed often, and so the time periods of his work are labeled in this way. A few of the many names that he used were; Shunrō, Tawaraya Sōri, Hokusai Tomisa, Katsushika Hokusai, Taito, Litsu, Gakyō Rōjin Manji etc.

In 1807 Hokusai worked with the well-known novelist Takizawa Bakin on a collection of illustrated books. He also later created the *Hokusai Manga* and a variety of art manuals filled with thousands of drawings. Hokusai reached the peak of his career in the 1820s. His most famous work, *Thirty-Six Views of Mount Fuji*, would include his well-known illustration of the *Great Wave off Kanagawa*.

Hokusai was married twice in his lifetime. Both marriages were quite brief with the two wives dying shortly after the marriages. He had two sons and three daughters with these wives. His youngest daughter, Sakae, later became an artist, following in her father's footsteps.

Continually painting all throughout his long life, it is said that, on his deathbed, Hokusai exclaimed, "If only Heaven will give me just another ten years... Just another five more years, then I could become a real painter." Katsushika Hokusai died on May 10, 1849 at the age of 89, and was laid to rest in his native city, Tokyo.

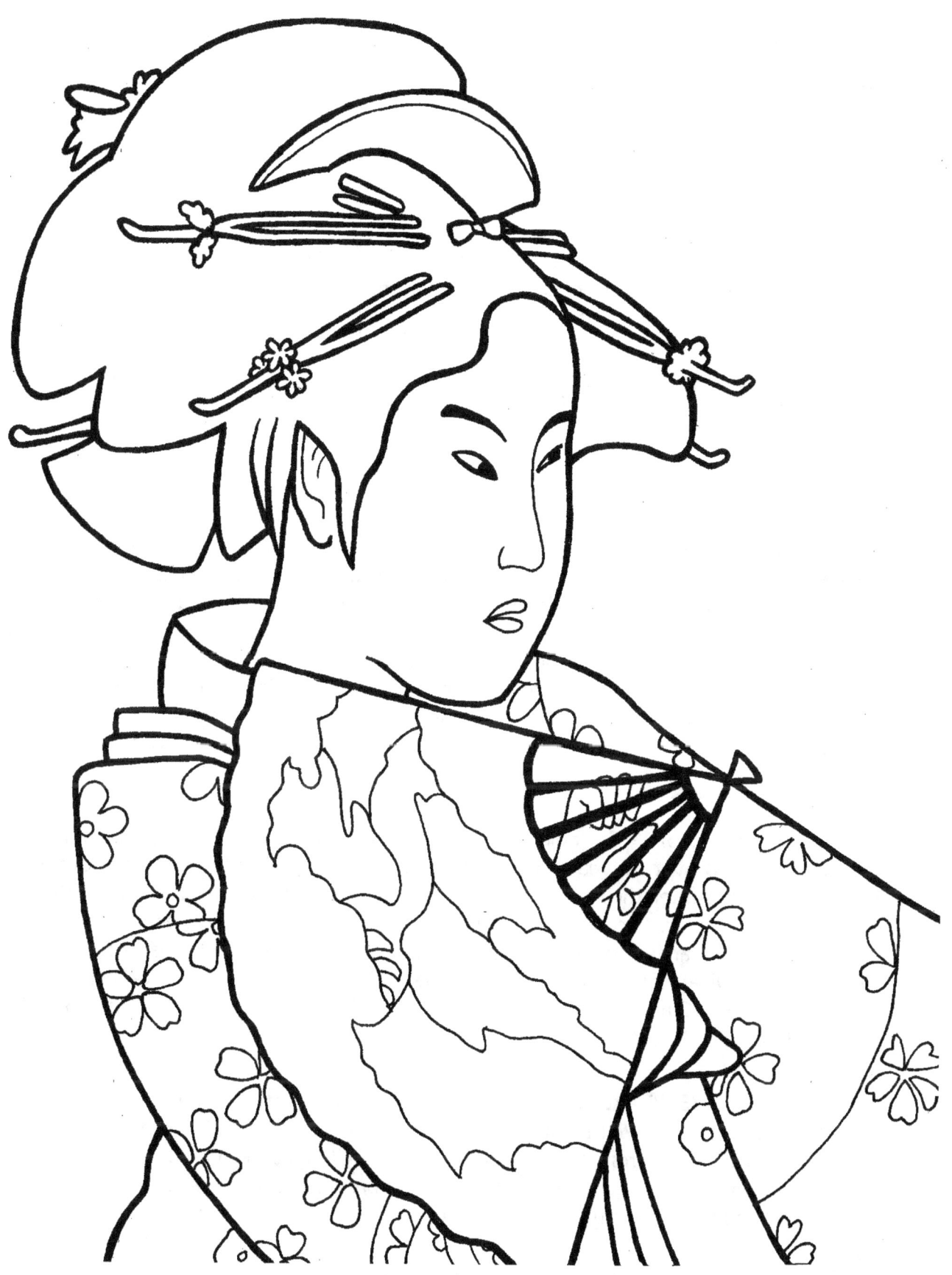

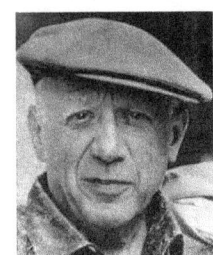

Pablo Picasso
(October 25, 1881 – April 8, 1973)

🎨 Pablo Ruiz y Picasso was born on October 25, 1881 in the city of Málaga, Spain. His parents were Don José Ruiz y Blasco and María Picasso y López. He had two younger sisters, Lola and Concepción (aka Conchita, who died at the age of seven). His father was a painter, a professor of art and the curator of a local museum.

🎨 Picasso's interest in art began early in life. At the age of seven, he began formal training with his father, working in oil painting and figure drawing. At the age of 13, he would attend the Barcelona School of Fine Arts. At age 16, he attended Madrid's Royal Academy of San Fernando. Picasso never enjoyed the formal training process and so he left these schools soon after enrollment, seeking artistic freedom.

🎨 Picasso's art is categorized by color periods, where his artwork favored different hues for each span of time. His *Blue Period* (1901 to 1904) was a time when Picasso favored painting in shades of blue, depicting emaciated mothers with children, prostitutes and beggars. Picasso's *Rose Period* (1904 to 1906) was when he chose to explore a brighter and more cheerful pallet, featuring more orange and pink color. The favored subjects during this time were circus people, acrobats and harlequins. His *Crystal Period* (1915 to 1917) was when Picasso began working in a highly geometric style, with minimalist Cubist objects; "Hard-edged square-cut diamonds", is how art historian, John Richardson, had described his work. [1]

🎨 In the summer of 1918, Pablo Picasso was wed to Olga Khokhlova, a ballerina. Their marriage spanned over 37 years, but the two were not together for the entire duration. In fact, only 9 years after they had wed, the two were separated due to Pablo's affair with Marie-Thérèse Walter. Because Picasso did not want to lose any property in a divorce, he remained legally married to Khokhlova until her death in 1955. Pablo had one son, Paulo, with his wife, Olga; he had one daughter, Maya, with his mistress, Marie-Thérèse; and he had two children, Claude and Paloma, with his girlfriend Françoise Gilot. In 1961, Picasso married Jacqueline Roque.

🎨 On April 8, 1973, Picasso and his wife, Jacqueline, were entertaining guests at their hilltop villa of Notre Dame de Vie. During dinner, the 91-year-old artist died suddenly from heart failure. He was laid to rest on his property at the Chateau de Vauvenargues, in France. Jacqueline never fully recovered from her husband's death, the grief and loneliness eventually driving her to commit suicide in 1986.

🎨 Picasso is portrayed in the 1996 film, *Surviving Picasso,* starring Anthony Hopkins, Natasha McElhone, Julianne Moore, Joseph Maher and Joan Plowright.

The Old Guitarist (c. 1903-04) by Pablo Picasso

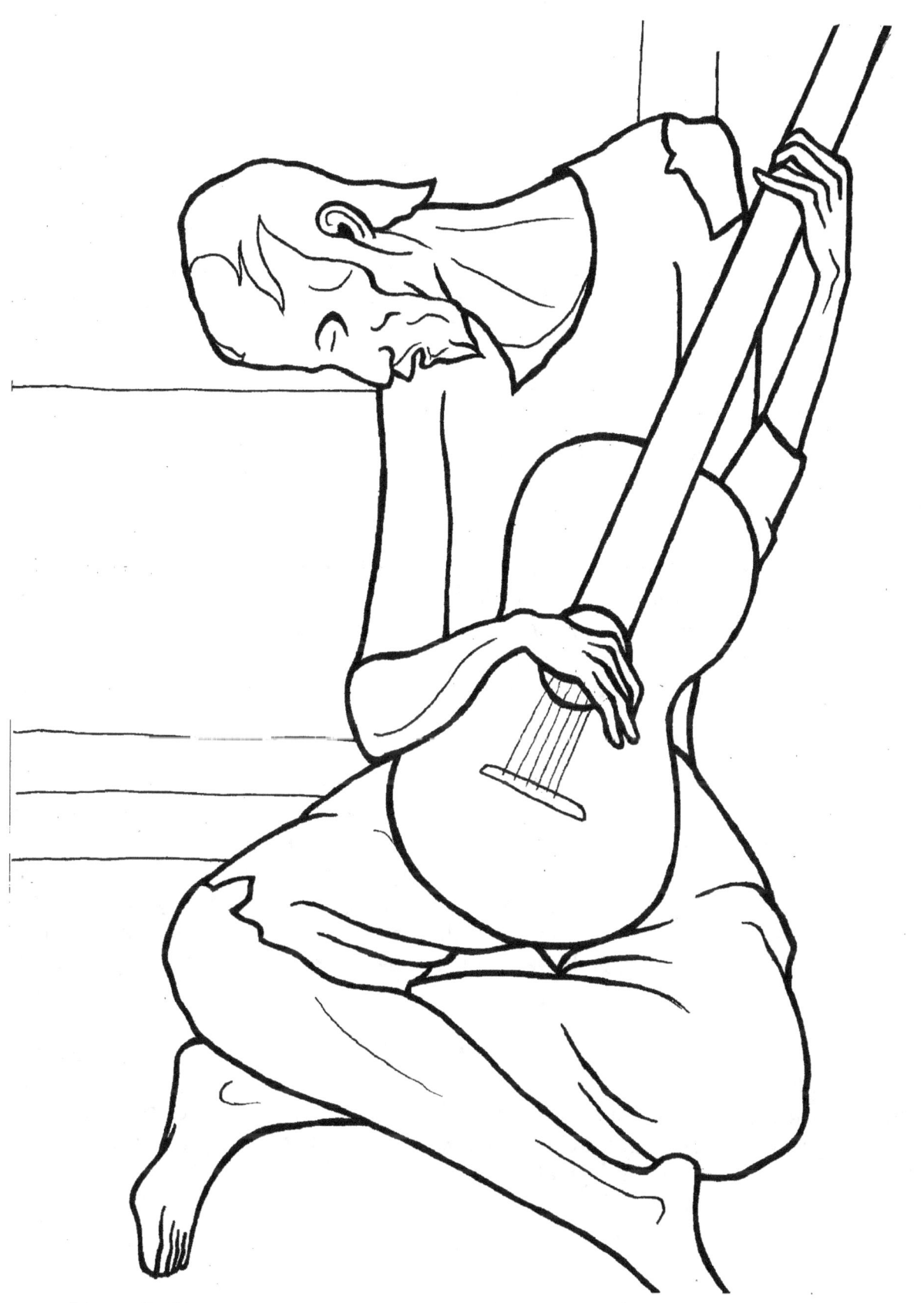

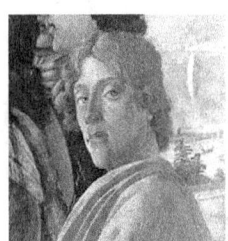

Sandro Botticelli
(c. 1445 – May 17, 1510)

Alessandro di Mariano di Vanni Filipepi, also known as Sandro Botticelli, was born in the city of Florence around 1445; the exact date is unknown. His father was Mariano di Vanni d'Amedeo Filipepi and his mother was Smeralda Filipepi. He had three siblings; Giovannii, Antonio and Simone.

An Italian painter of the Early Renaissance, Botticelli was initially trained as a goldsmith by his brother Antonio. By 1462, he was apprenticed to Fra Filippo Lippi, one of the finest artists of his time. Having been only around fourteen years old, at the time, would mean that Botticelli would receive a more extensive education than most other Renaissance artists. By 1470, Botticelli had his own workshop.

In the summer of 1481, Pope Sixtus IV requested that Botticelli and a team of other well-known local painters come to fresco the walls of the Sistine Chapel. Botticelli contributed four paintings to this project; St. *Sixtus II, Punishment of Korah, Dathan and Abiram, The Temptation of Christ* and *The Trials of Moses*. After this impressive display, Botticelli was promoted and financially backed by one of the most respected patrons of the Renaissance arts - Lorenzo de Medici.

Botticelli never took a wife. In fact, he expressed a complete aversion to the thought of marriage. It is popularly believed that he was infatuated with a married noblewoman, Simonetta Vespucci, and would have no other. Simonetta was Botticelli's model and muse for *The Birth of Venus*, one of Botticelli's most memorable pieces. Her image was his inspiration for this painting, and many others, even though she had died years earlier, in 1476. Botticelli requested that upon his death, he be buried at her feet in the Church of Ognissanti in Florence. This final wish was granted when he died, around the age of 65, in the year 1510.

After death, Botticelli's reputation faded into the shadows for a time, much longer than that of any other major European artist. His paintings lived on in their places within the churches and other locations, though his work in the Sistine Chapel was much overshadowed by Michelangelo's contributions. Obviously, his work did find its way back into the light of public eye over time, as one of the great masters.

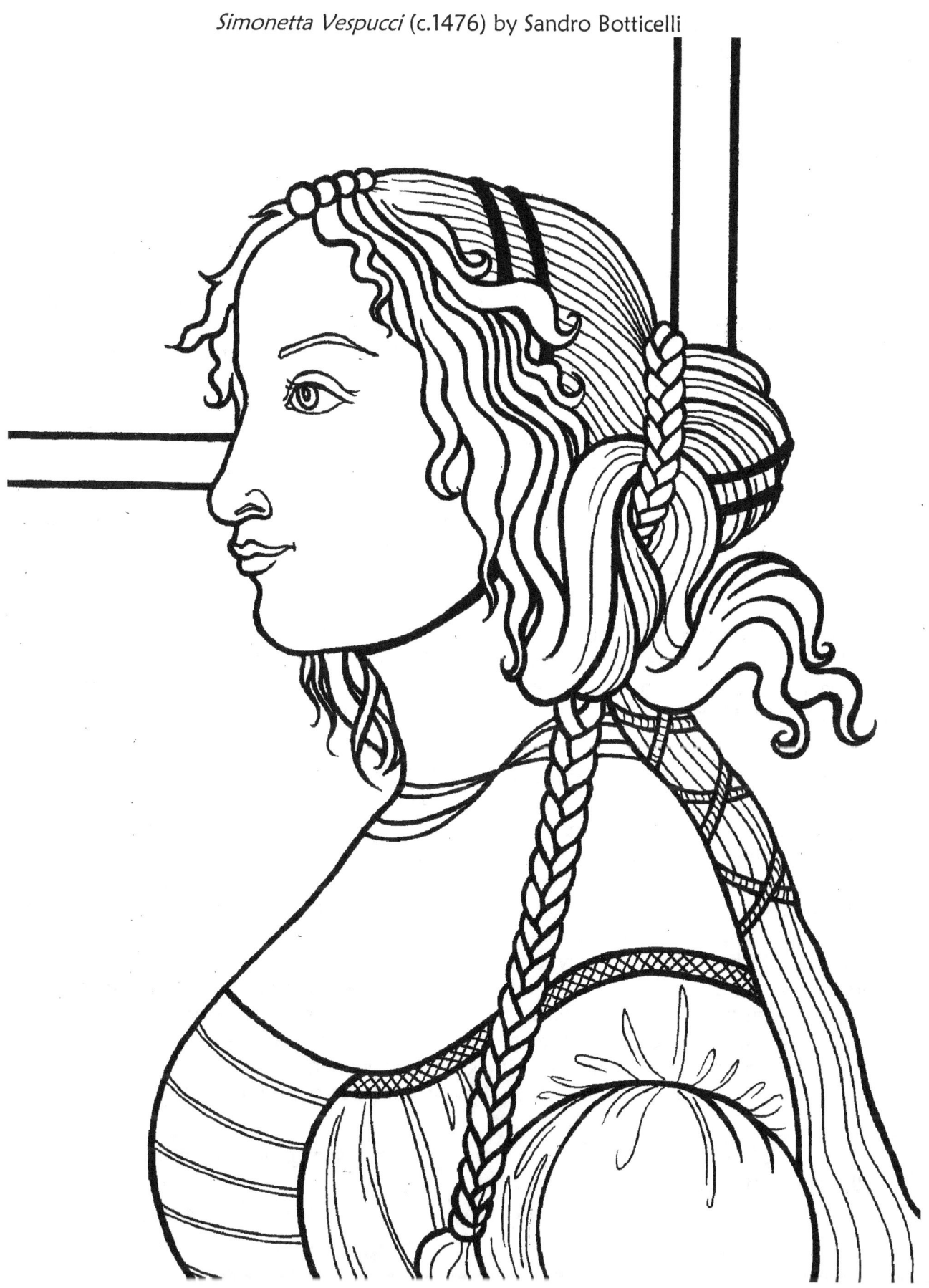

Simonetta Vespucci (c.1476) by Sandro Botticelli

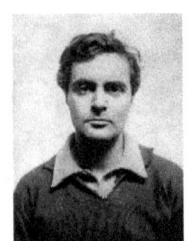

Amedeo Modigliani
(July 12, 1884 – January 24, 1920)

Amedeo Clemente Modigliani was born in Livorno, Italy on July 12, 1884. He was the fourth child of Flaminio Modigliani and Eugénie Garsin, It is said, that he saved his family from complete ruin upon his birth. According to an old law, debt collectors could not seize the bed of a pregnant woman or a new mother. As luck would have it, Eugénie went into labor as the creditors arrived in their home and the family saved a great deal of their valued possessions by piling them on the bed with her and the newly born Amedeo.

Amedeo began formal training around the age of 14 with the painting master, Guglielmo Micheli. Around 1902 he enrolled in the Scuola Libera di Nudo, of the Accademia di Belle Arti in Florence. A year later he enrolled at the Regia Accademia ed Istituto di Belle Arti, in Venice; all while actively battling tuberculosis. Modigliani worked as a painter and sculptor throughout his lifetime. His work in portraiture is characterized by the focus that he put on elongating the subject's neck and faces.

In 1917, Modigliani was introduced to Jeanne Hébuterne. The two became romantically involved, moving together into a studio on the Rue de la Grande Chaumière. Jeanne became the main subject for many of the artist's paintings. The couple had one daughter, Jeanne Modigliani (1918-1984)

After an attack of pleurisy around the age of 11, Amedeo had suffered from a multitude of health problems throughout his life. In 1906 Modigliani moved to Paris, settling into a commune for penniless artists in Montmartre. It was here that Modigliani began to use alcohol and drugs more excessively in attempt to alleviate the pains of his illness as it reached the final stages. He battled a second bout of pleurisy, typhoid fever and finally tuberculosis. Amedeo Modigliani finally succumbed to his illness, dying on January 24, 1920, at the Hôpital de la Charité. Jeanne was 8 months pregnant with their second child at the time. After a grand funeral, she was taken to her parent's house where, a day later, she threw herself out of a fifth-floor window killing both her and their unborn child. Modigliani was buried in Père Lachaise Cemetery, while Hébuterne was buried at the Cimetière de Bagneux, near Paris. Years later, in 1930, Jeanne's family relented, allowing her body to be moved and laid to rest beside Modigliani. A single headstone marks the lover's tomb; for Modigliani, the epitaph reads: "Struck down by Death at the moment of glory" and Jeanne's reads: "Devoted companion to the extreme sacrifice".

Modigliani is portrayed in the film of the same name, *Modigliani;* starring Andy Garcia, Elsa Zylberstein, Peter Capaldi, Udo Kier etc.

Jeanne Hebuterne with Hat and Necklace (1917) by Amedeo Modigliani

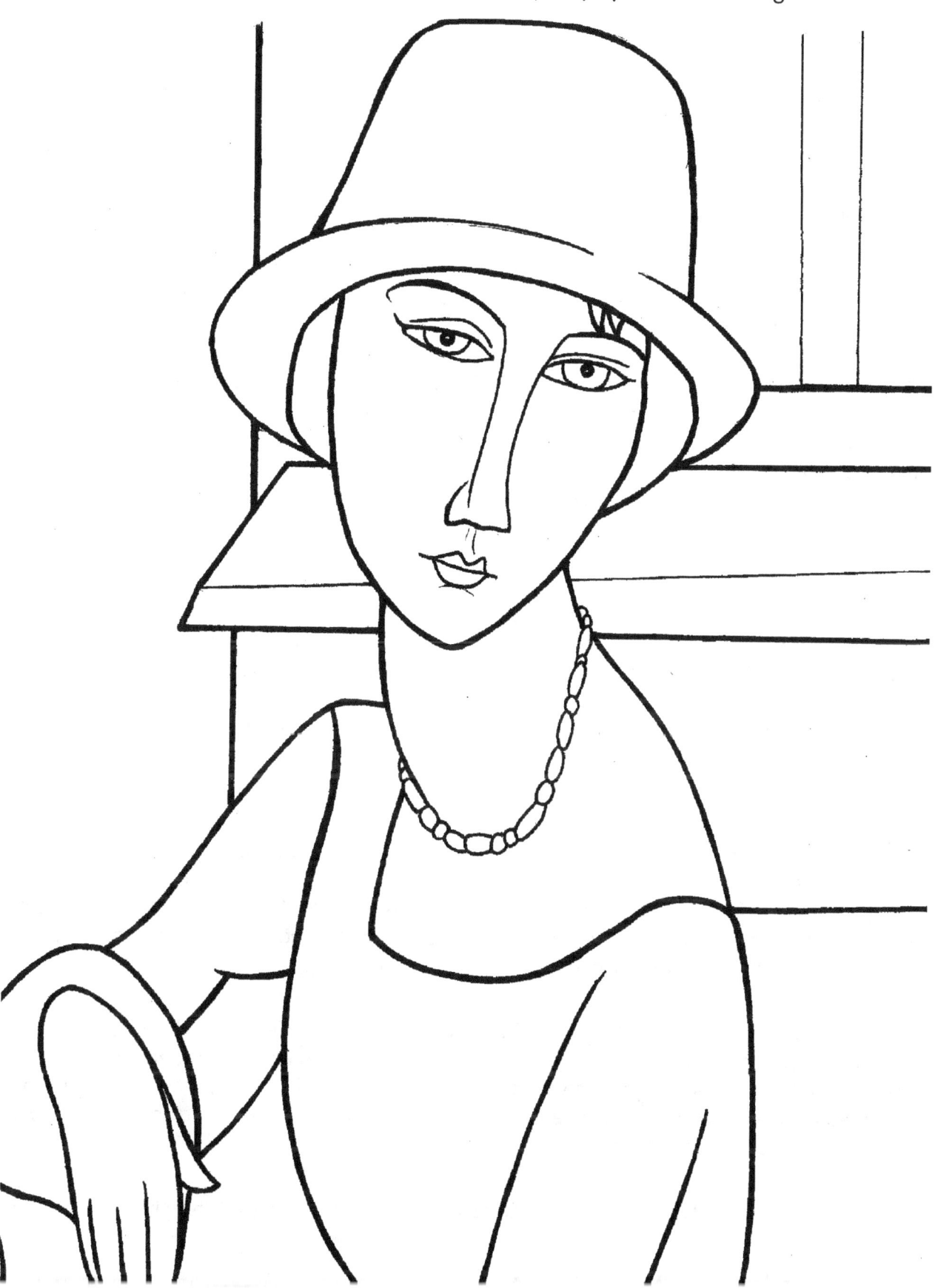

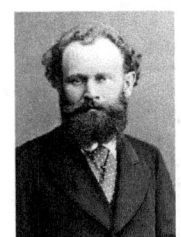

Edouard Manet
(January 23, 1832 – April 30, 1883)

🎨 Édouard Manet was born in Paris on January 23, 1832, to his parents, Eugénie-Desirée Fournier and Auguste Manet. Their family held an upper-class status, with Manet's mother being the daughter of a diplomat as well as the goddaughter of the Swedish crown prince Charles Bernadotte; his father was well esteemed as a French judge. Edouard Manet had two brothers, Eugene and Gustav.

🎨 Manet's father expected that he would follow in his footsteps, pursuing a career in law; however, his uncle, Edmond Fournier, had different aspirations for the boy. He saw the child's natural artistic talent and encouraged young Manet to hone his skills through painting. In 1845, Manet followed his uncle's advice and enrolled in an art class at his school. This is where he would meet the future Minister of Fine Arts, Antonin Proust, who would become his lifelong friend. After failing twice in the examination to join the Navy, Manet's father finally accepted his sons path in art.

🎨 Manet was one of the first artists, of his time, to illustrate modern life in his artwork; transitioning from Realism to Impressionism. He illustrated everyday social scenes including such works as *The café concert*, *The luncheon* and *Music in the Tuileries*. He also painted more intimate portraits and nudes. Manet focused a variety of his work on depictions of war, such as *The execution of Emperor Maximillian* and *The battle of Cherbourg*. In 1875, Manet contributed lithographs that were included in the French edition of Edgar Allan Poe's *The Raven*.

🎨 In 1863, Manet married Suzanne Leenhoff, a Dutch-born piano teacher who had originally been hired by Manet's father to teach him and his younger brother how to play the piano. In 1852, eleven years earlier, Suzanne had given birth to a son, Leon Koella Leenhoff. It was uncertain if this child, being born out of wedlock, was in fact Édouard's biological son. Young Leon often posed for Manet's paintings.

🎨 Sometime in his forties Manet was infected with syphilis. He received no treatment for this illness and, in addition, suffered from rheumatism. He lived in considerable pain from these afflictions and their progressive side-effects. In 1883 he had to have his left foot amputated because of gangrene; he died less than a fortnight afterward in Paris and was buried in the Passy Cemetery of Paris, France.

🎨 Manet is portrayed in the 2006 film, *Manet in Love;* starring Shelley Philips, Alyssa Bresnaham, Clement von Franckenstein.

The Café Concert (c. 1879) by Eduard Manet

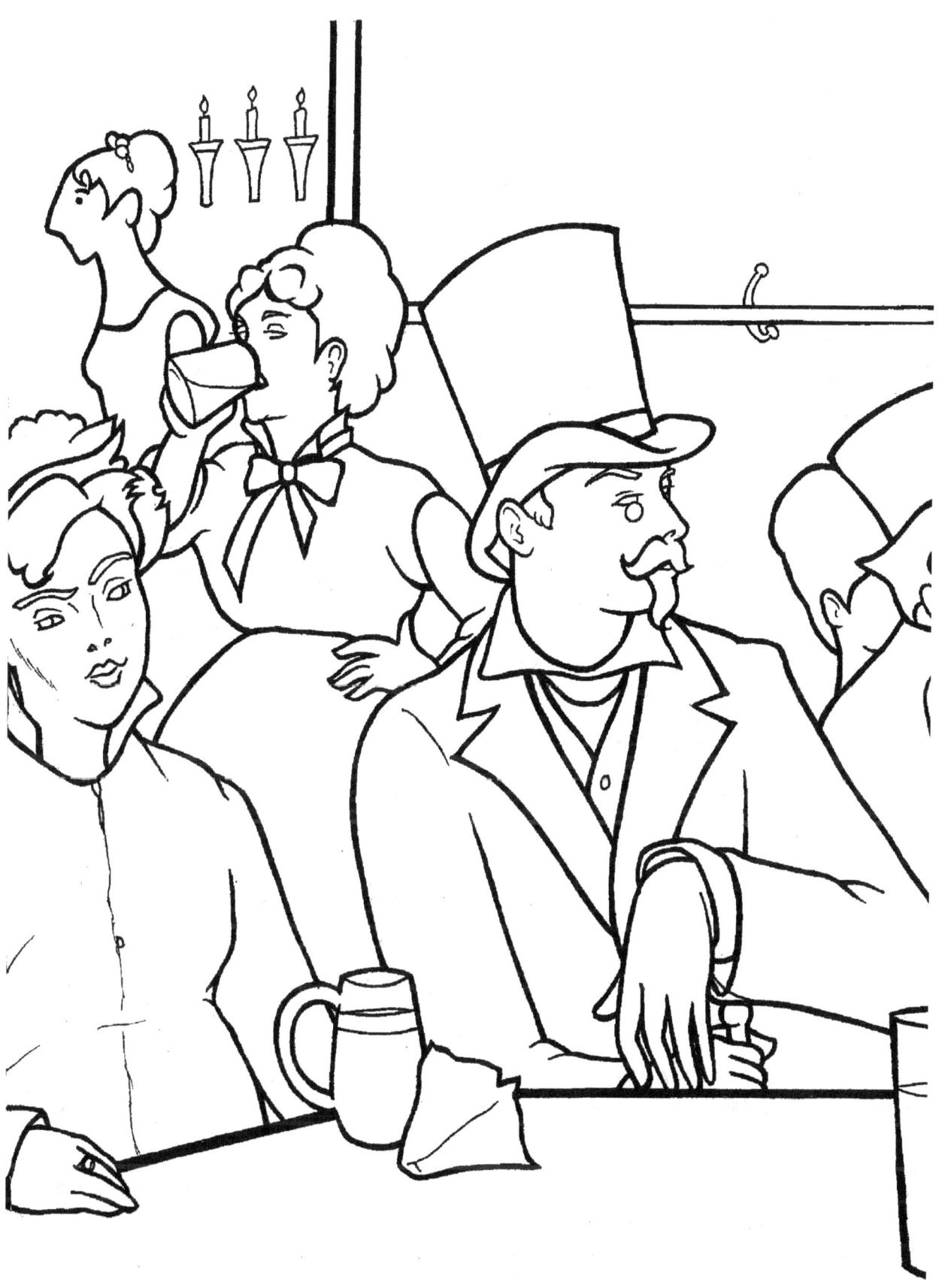

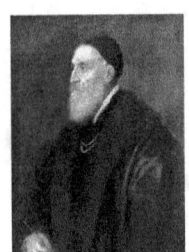

Titian
(c.1488/1490 – August 27, 1576)

🎨 Tiziano Vecelli, known as Titian, was born in Pieve di Cadore, Northern italy. The exact date of his birth is unknown, but most scholars believe it to be sometime between 1488 and 1490. His father, Gregorio Vecelli, was distinguished as the superintendent for the castle of Pieve di Cadore and as a soldier. His mother was Lucia Vecelli. Titian was the oldest of four children.

🎨 In his early teens, Titian and his brother, Francesco, were both sent to their uncle in Venice to seek an apprenticeship with a painter. The boys began training with Sebastian Zuccato, and later with Giovanni Bellini, the most notable artists in the area at that time. Titian painted many masterpieces in these early years, but his *Assumption of the Virgin*, an altarpiece for the church of Santa Maria Gloriosa dei Frari, is the work that brought him into the spotlight as the leading artists of his time. Outliving his teachers, Titian became the master of Venetian painting.

🎨 Titian was quite the dynamic artist, being very versatile in his subject matter. He demonstrated equal skill in the area of portraits, landscape, mythological and religious themes. His method of painting, especially the way he used color, would be profoundly influential not only on the painters of his time, but also in future generations around the world. You can see examples of his vivid use of color in works such as, *A man with a quilted sleeve* and *Bacchus and Ariadne.*

🎨 With his innovative use of brilliant colors, his fascinating choice of composition and his loose style of brushwork, Titian has been a most profound influence in the art world. He has inspired many generations of artists, including notable artists such as Rembrandt and Caravaggio, among others.

🎨 Titian married Cecilia, a woman who had been his housekeeper and mistress for many years. She gave Titian two healthy sons, Pomponio and Orazio, while out of wedlock. In 1525 when she became seriously ill, Titian chose to legitimize their children and married her immediately. Cecilia recovered and they went on to have quite a happy marriage, including two more children; his daughter Lavinia and another who died in infancy. Cecilia died in August of 1530. Titian never remarried.

🎨 Titian lived well into his 80s, before dying on August 27, 1576. Some sources report that he died of old age and some say that he died of plague, as the dark illness was in fact ravaging the city of Venice during this time. The much-celebrated artist was interred in the Basilica di Santa Maria Gloriosa dei Frari, where two of his most famous works may still be seen on display.

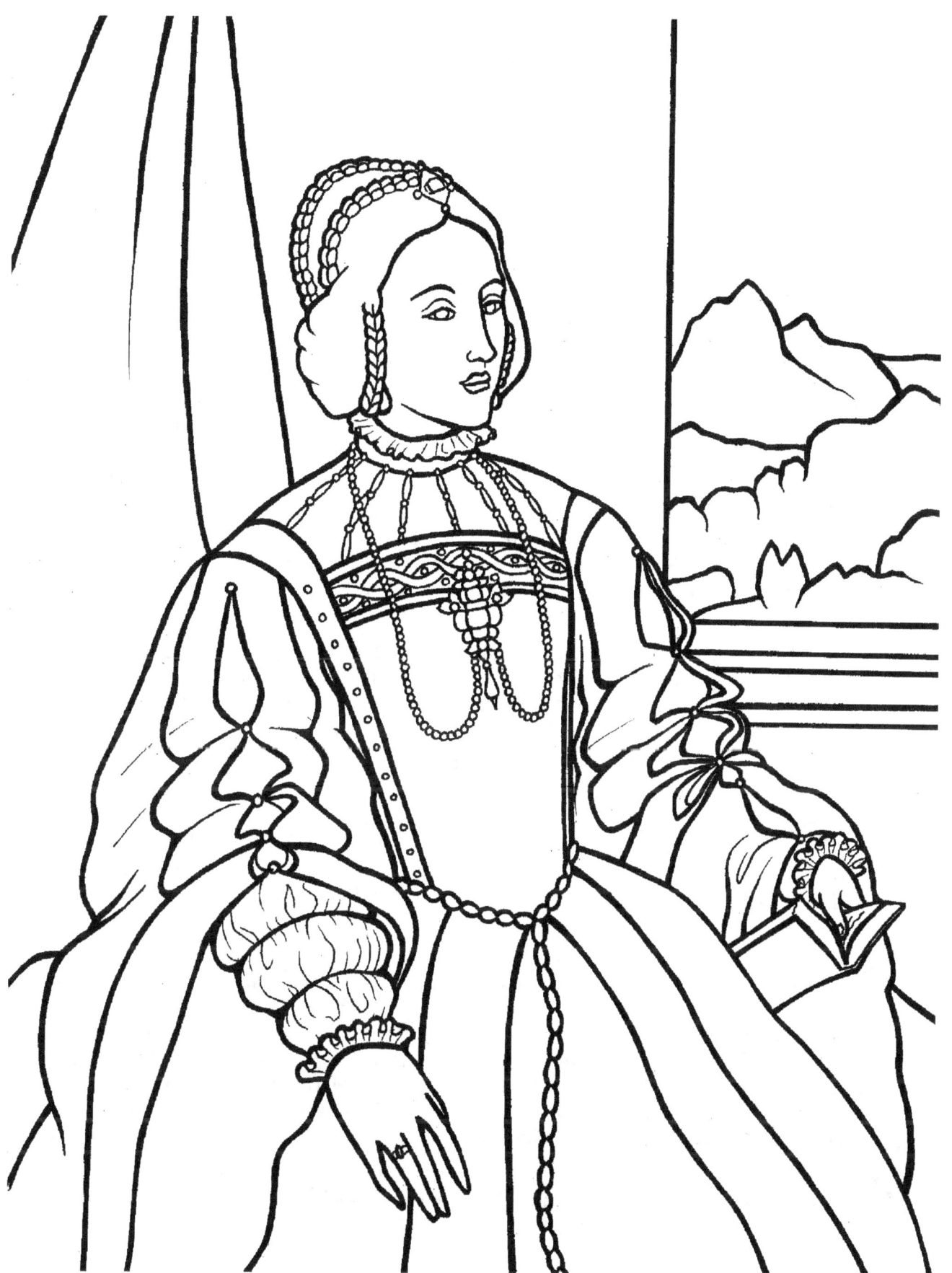

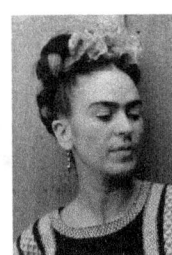

Frida Khalo
(July 6, 1907 – July 13, 1954)

Magdalena Carmen Frida Kahlo y Calderón was born in Coyoacán, Mexico on July 6, 1907. Her father, Guillermo Kahlo, was a German-Mexican photographer; her mother was Matilde Calderón y González, a woman of both Spanish and Mexican descent. Frida had three sisters; Christina, Adriana and Matilde.

Frida had originally been a student of medicine but, after a tragic accident, she was bedridden in a body cast for months and turned to painting to fill her time. She had no formal training and was self-taught, with the encouraging and helpful comments of Diego Rivera greatly influencing her development as an artist.

Frida's artwork is internationally recognized as the epitome of Mexican culture, and by women worldwide for its strong depiction of the female form and emotion. She is best known for her many self-portraits, which vividly illustrated her pain and emotion. Frida once said, "I paint myself because I am so often alone and because I am the subject I know best."

At the age of eighteen, Frida was in a terrible bus accident where she suffered numerous injuries including a broken spinal column, ribs, collarbone and pelvis, multiple fractures in her right leg, a dislocated shoulder and a crushed, dislocated foot. Her lower right leg was eventually amputated for gangrene. However, of all these, the injury that truly haunted her was the iron handrail that had pierced her body, impaling her uterus and taking away any hope of her ever carrying a child.

In her journey as an artist, Frida met and fell madly in love with the Mexican muralist, Diego Rivera. Their relationship was a tumultuous one, with repeated infidelity on both sides; the most damaging affair was with Frida's sister. In 1939 the couple divorced, only to remarry in 1940, although their second marriage was no different from the first. They kept separate living quarters adjacent to each other.

Frida Khalo died on July 13, 1954 at the age of 47, leaving a message in her diary that read, "I hope the exit is joyful and I hope never to return - Frida". Her cause of death was originally recorded as a pulmonary embolism, though no autopsy was performed. Sadly, it was not until after Frida's death that Diego Rivera realized the depth of his love for her, as he later lamented in his autobiography. Frida's remains are respectfully kept in an urn which is on display in her family home, La Casa Azul (The Blue House), in Coyoacán, Mexico. La Casa Azul is now maintained as a museum with numerous pieces of her art and mementos.

Frida is portrayed in the 2002 film of the same name, *Frida;* starring Salma Hayek as the artist and Alfred Molina as her husband, Diego Rivera.

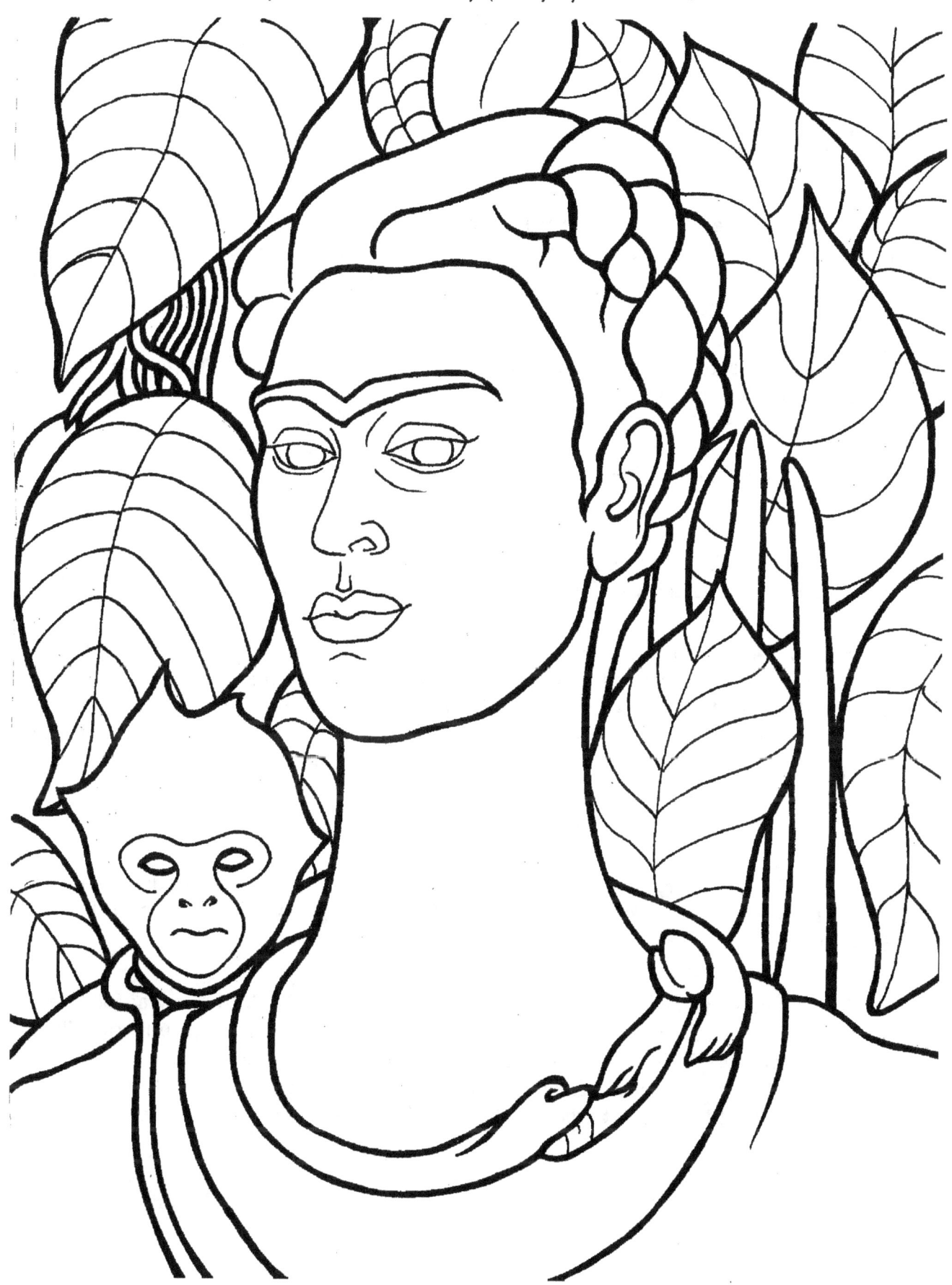

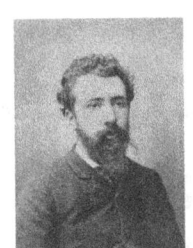

Georges Seurat
(December 2, 1859 – March 29, 1891)

Georges Pierre Seurat was born in Paris on December 2, 1859. His father, Antoine Chrysostome Seurat, was a legal official who later became wealthy through property investments; his mother was Ernestine Faivre. Seurat had two older siblings; his brother, Émile Augustin, and his sister, Marie-Berthe.

Seurat's formal training in art began with his studies at the École Municipale de Sculpture et Dessin (the Municipal school of Sculpture and drawing), near his home in Paris. He later attended the École des Beaux-Arts (school of fine arts), where he was instructed by Henri Lehmann; a German-born historical painter and portrait artist. His formal training in art ended with his military enlistment in 1879.

Georges Seurat is best known for creating the art forms now known as chromoluminarism/Divisionism and pointillism; techniques in painting where dots or patches of color are used repeatedly to form a completed image.

In 1890, Seurat wrote a letter to his friend, Maurice Beaubourg, a French journalist: "Art is Harmony. Harmony is the analogy of the contrary and of similar elements of tone, of colour and of line. In tone, lighter against darker. In colour, the complementary, red-green, orange-blue, yellow-violet. In line, those that form a right-angle. The frame is in a harmony that opposes those of the tones, colours and lines of the picture, these aspects are considered according to their dominance and under the influence of light, in gay, calm or sad combinations". (*Art of the 20th century*, by Karl Ruhrberg)

Seurat did not marry in his lifetime, but he did live with one of his models, Madeleine Knobloch. The couple had one child together, Pierre-Georges, who was born on February 16, 1890.

Seurat died when he was only 31 years of age, on March 29, 1891. He was followed in death by his son, who passed away only two weeks later, taken by the same unknown illness. At the time of Seurat's death, Madeleine had been pregnant with their second son, but the child died soon after his birth. Seurat was laid to rest at Cimetière du Père-Lachaise on the 31st day of March 1891. His last great work, *The Circus*, was sadly left unfinished.

Le chahut (c.1889-90) by Georges Seurat

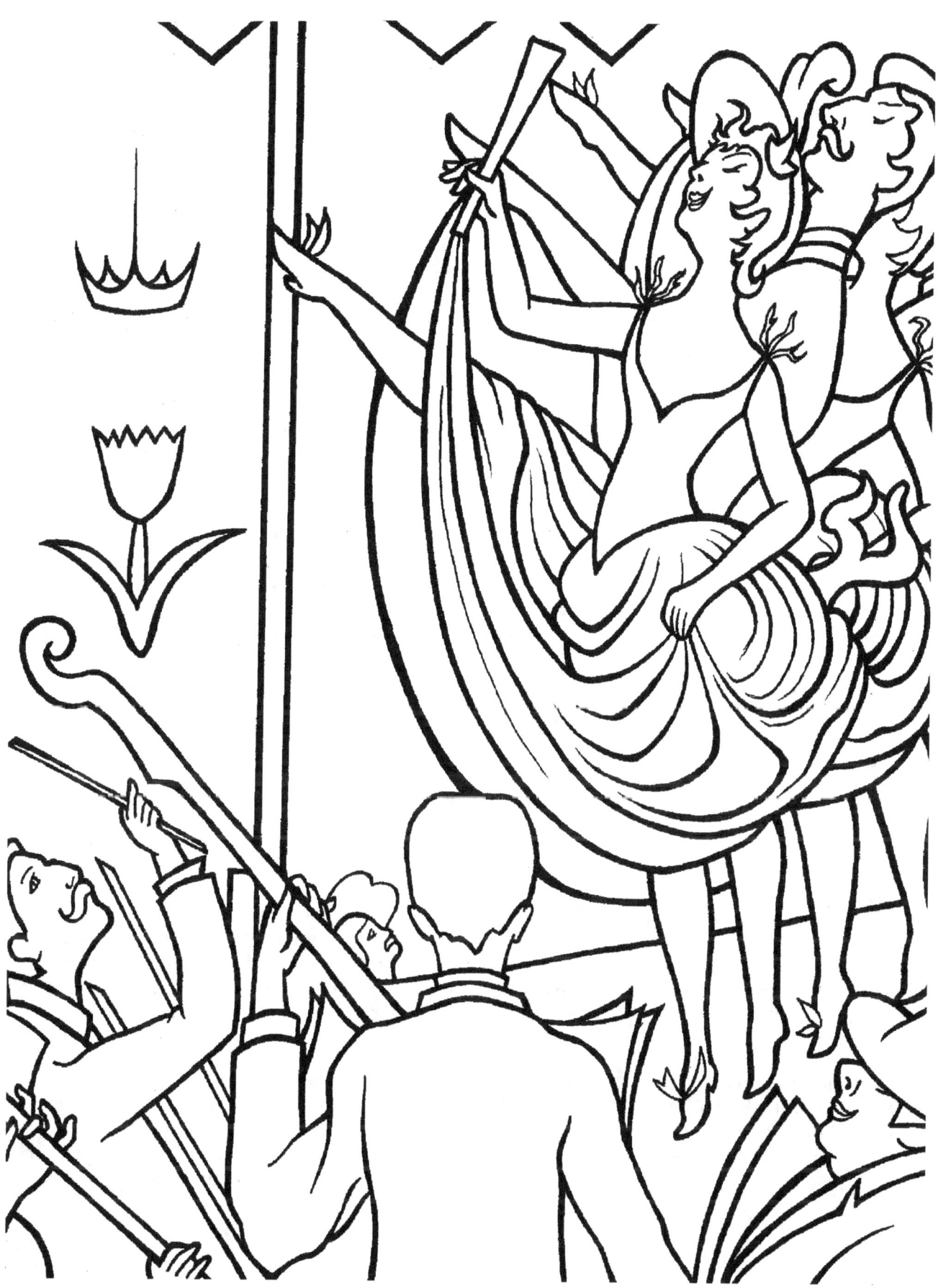

Edvard Munch

(December 12, 1863 – January 23, 1944)

Edvard Munch was born on December 12, 1863 in the village of Ådalsbruk in Løten, Norway. His father, Christian Munch, was a doctor; his mother was Laura Catherine Bjølstad. Edvard had one older sister, Johanne Sophie, and three younger siblings, Peter Andreas, Inger Marie and Laura Catherine.

Munch showed an interest in art from a young age, drawing to keep himself entertained during the months that he was kept out of school due to illness, which was quite often. In 1881 Munch began his studies at the Royal School of Art and Design of Kristiania, under the tutelage of Julius Middelthun (sculptor) and Christian Krohg (painter).

Edvard Munch experimented with many art styles throughout his career, working to hone his individual style. In the earlier stages of his exploration, Munch's work was somewhere between *Naturalistic* and *Impressionistic*, though he later was known for subject matter that was more *Symbolist*, depicting the inner landscapes of emotion and thought, rather than the external, physical world around him. *The Scream* is a good example of these inner landscapes; Edvard described the inspiration for this piece after a stroll as, "…I sensed a scream passing through nature; it seemed to me that I heard the scream. I painted this picture, painted the clouds as actual blood. The color shrieked. This became the scream."['] [35]

In 1940, when the Germans invaded Norway, 76-year-old Munch lived in fear that the Nazis would confiscate his work, as he kept a large collection in his house. Many of his paintings were in fact taken by the Nazis, but were later returned to Norway through purchases made by collectors, including *The Scream* and *The Sick Child.* These pieces were later housed in public galleries.

Munch never married and he had no children. His lived a life of solitude, a life that was filled with hardship, illness and sorrow. Both his mother and his favorite sister died when he was young, a lasting source of grief for him. He once said, in speaking of life and of his father, "…From him I inherited the seeds of madness. The angels of fear, sorrow and death stood by my side since the day I was born. [']"

Munch battled with ill health for most of his life, and later combined this with anxiety and alcoholism. In 1908, Munch had a breakdown as his drinking habits become quite severe; he was treated and stabilized through therapy. Munch eventually succumbed to Pneumonia along with Cardiovascular disease and died on January 23, 1944, at the age of 80, in his home at Ekely. His works were donated to the Norwegian government and placed in various museums in Norway.

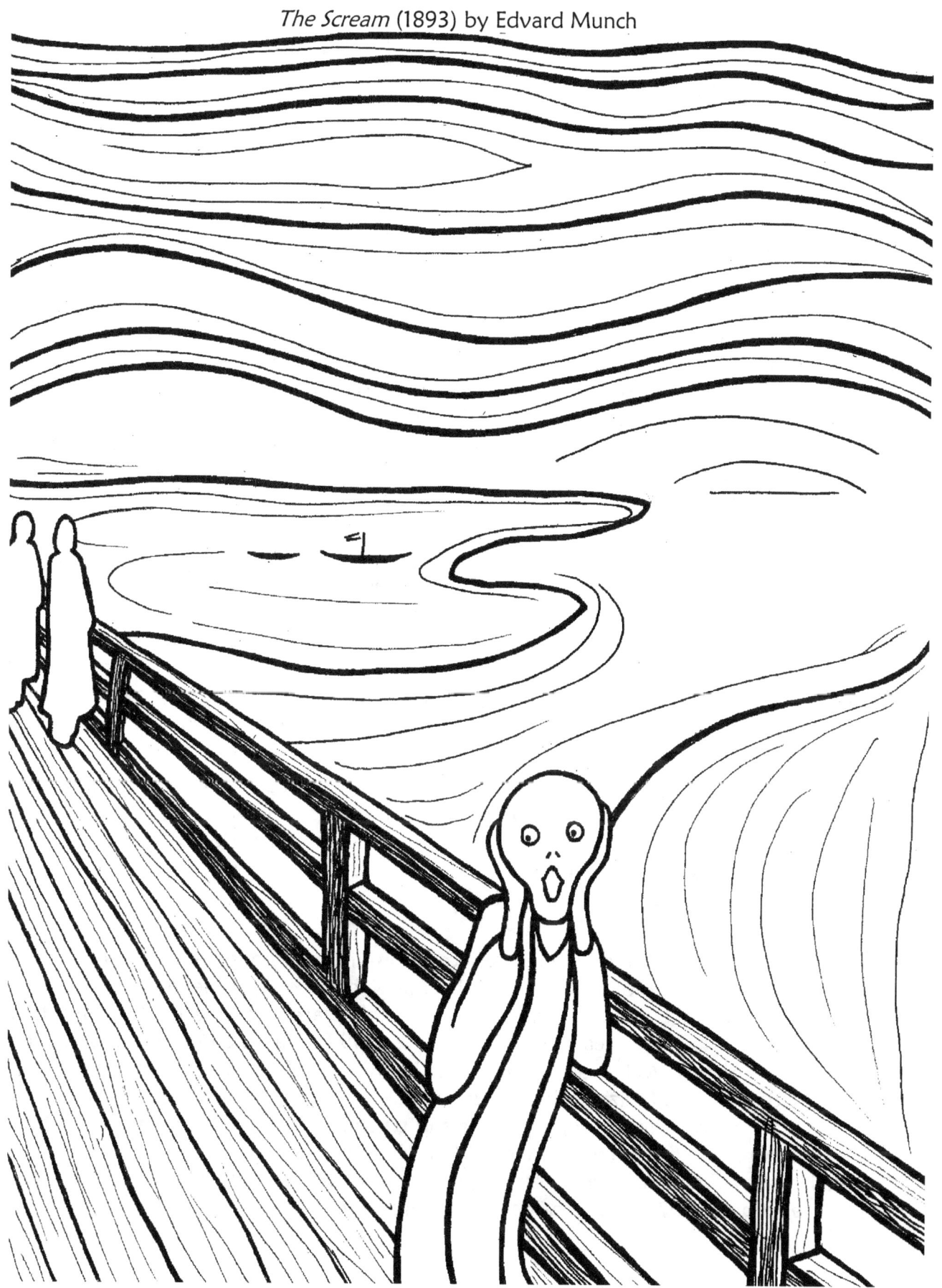

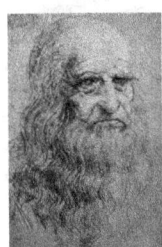

Leonardo da Vinci
(April 15, 1452 – May 2, 1519)

🎨 Leonardo di ser Piero da Vinci was born on April 15, 1452. His father, Messer Piero Fruosino di Antonio da Vinci, was a wealthy legal notary. His mother was a peasant woman named Caterina. Leonardo was born outside of wedlock, and so he was given no surname; da Vinci simply means "From Vinci" (Vinci, Tuscany). However, he is named for his father in his full birth name, Lionardo di ser Piero da Vinci, meaning "Leonardo, son of Piero from Vinci" [1]. Leonardo lived with his mother until he was five and then he went to live with his father where he eventually had 12 half-siblings!

🎨 Leonardo began his career in art at the age of fourteen, with his apprenticeship to the artist Andrea di Cione, known as Verrocchio. By the age of twenty, Leonardo was a master in the Guild of Saint Luke, a guild of artists and practitioners of medicine. His career led him to be well-known and sought after; often commissioned to paint for monasteries, chapels and cathedrals. His beautifully rendered paintings are what he is best known for today, however, Leonardo had a large range of other talents that he was often employed for, such as; sculpting, map making, architecture and, of course, his many inventions.

🎨 Leonardo, more than merely an artist, was also greatly valued as an engineer. He created a system of moveable barricades to protect the city of Venice; He built musical instruments such as the silver Lyre in the shape of a horse's head crafted for Ludovico Sforza, Duke of Milan. He also designed things that were decidedly before his time, such as his "flying machines" and parachutes.

🎨 In 1516, Leonardo entered the last service of his lifetime, along with his pupil, Count Francesco Melzi. By order of King Francis I, he was given the use of the manor house *Clos Lucé*, near to the king's own residence. It was in this place, working for the king, that Leonardo spent his last three years of life. On May 2, 1519 Leonardo da Vinci died of natural causes at the age of 67. As he had no wife or children in his lifetime, Leonardo deemed his closest friend and pupil, Melzi, as the executor of his will and as the main heir to his estate; receiving his money, paintings, library, tools and personal effects. He named a servant, as well as another pupil, to each receive a half of his vineyards; and his brothers to receive land as well. He *also left a fine coat to his serving woman. Leonardo's final resting place lies within in the Chapel of Saint-Hubert in Château d'Amboise, France.*

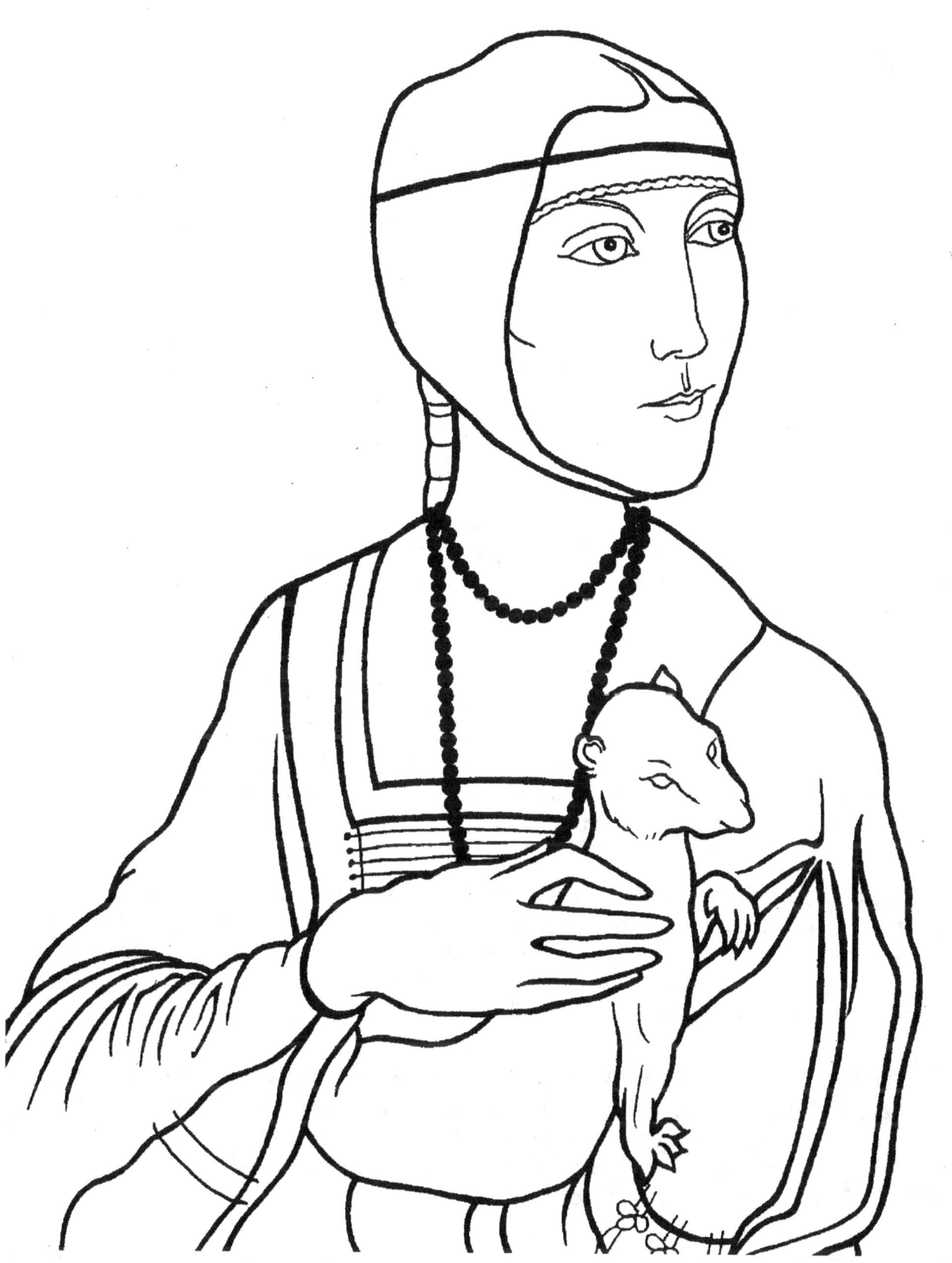

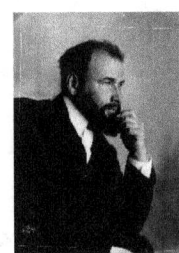

Gustav Klimt
(July 14, 1862 – February 6, 1918)

Gustav Klimt was born on July 14, 1862 in Baumgarten, Austria-Hungary. His father, Ernst Klimt, was a gold engraver; his mother was Anna Klimt. He had two brothers and four sisters.

Klimt, along with his two brothers, Ernst and Georg, all showed artistic talent early in life. Klimt studied architectural painting at the Vienna School of Arts and Crafts along with his brother Ernst, until 1883. During this time in school and afterwards, the two brothers, along with their friend, Franz Matsch, began taking on numerous commissions as a team. However, Klimt's artistic expression changed and evolved into a more solitary and personal style when both his father and his brother, Ernst, died in 1892.

Klimt is best known for his paintings, murals and particularly for his study of the female body. Much of his work was quite controversial at the time and was met with harsh criticism for its "pornographic" nature. For this reason, Gustav stopped taking public commissions and continued to paint privately.

There was a period of time in Klimt's career known as his "Golden Phase" or "Golden Period", where much of his paintings employed the use of gold leaf. This was the highlight of his career; a time when he received positive reactions from critics and a considerable increase in his income. His most widely known piece from this time period was called *The Kiss*. This painting is thought to be a portrayal of his long-time relationship with Emilie Flöge, though there is no record to prove this.

Gustav never married, though he is said to have fathered around 14 children throughout his lifetime. He did have a long-standing relationship with Emilie Louise Flöge, the sibling of his sister-in-law. Emilie was a successful business woman who owned a popular fashion salon. She was the muse for many of Klimt's paintings and would remain by his side until the day he died. Klimt's last words were, "Get Emilie".

After a long struggle with Pneumonia, followed by a stroke, Gustav Klimt died on February 6, 1918, at the age of 55. He is buried at the Hietzinger Cemetery in Hietzing, Vienna. His paintings continue to sell at some of the highest prices listed for artwork such as his. In 2006, the portrait of Adele Bloch-Bauer II (1912) was sold for $88 million; the portrait of Adele Bloch-Bauer I (1907) sold for $135 million!

Lady with a Fan (1918) by Gustav Klimt

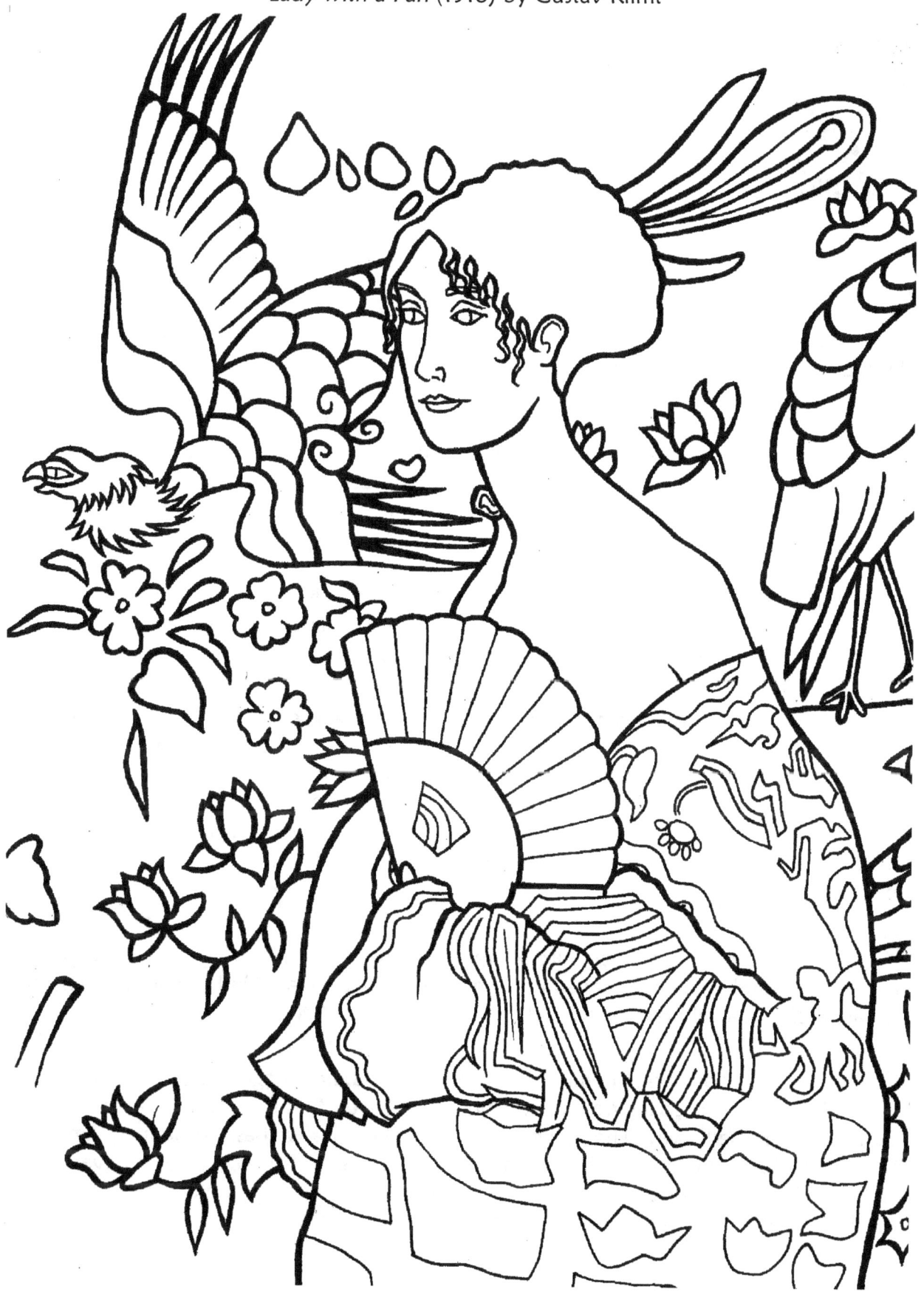

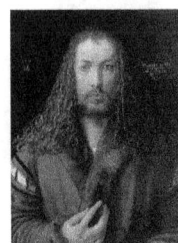

Albrecht Durer
(May 21, 1471 – April 6, 1528)

Albrecht Dürer was born on May 21, 1471 in Nuremburg of the Holy Roman Empire. His father, Albrecht Dürer the Elder, and his mother, Barbara Holper, had eighteen children, of which Albrecht was the second.

Albrecht and his brother, Hans Dürer, both became famous artists within their own lifetime. Albrecht established himself as an artist early in his twenties and was well-known for his woodcut prints, engravings, portraits and self-portraits, altarpieces, watercolors and for his books. Later in his career, he gained the patronage of the emperor himself, Maximilian I.

Dürer began his career as an artist at the age of fifteen, with an apprenticeship to Michael Wolgemut, a German painter and print maker. The apprenticeship began around 1486 and ended around 1490 when Albrecht began his *Wanderjahre*.

After completing his apprenticeship with Wolgemut, Albrecht followed the old custom known as *Wanderjahre* or "wandering years", also known as the Journeyman years. During the Wanderjahre (four years for Albrecht), the student must travel from town to town, learning from other masters in various workshops. The tradition of the Journeyman dates all the way back to medieval times and was a common part of the learning process for artists and craftsmen who wished to eventually become masters; it is still practiced today in some areas.

When Albrecht returned to Nuremberg, in July of 1494, at the age of 23, he entered the marriage that had been arranged for him while he was away. His bride was Agnes Frey, the daughter of a local brass worker. The couple had no children.

Albrecht Dürer died in Nuremburg, on April 6, 1528, at the age of 56. He was survived by his wife, who inherited his great estate, where she lived out the rest of her days until 1539, when she too passed away. The home is now a museum, as well as a prominent landmark of the area. Dürer is buried in the Johannisfriedhof cemetery of Nuremburg, Bavaria. The exact cause of Albrecht's death is unknown, but he did have an undetermined illness that stayed with him for many years until death.

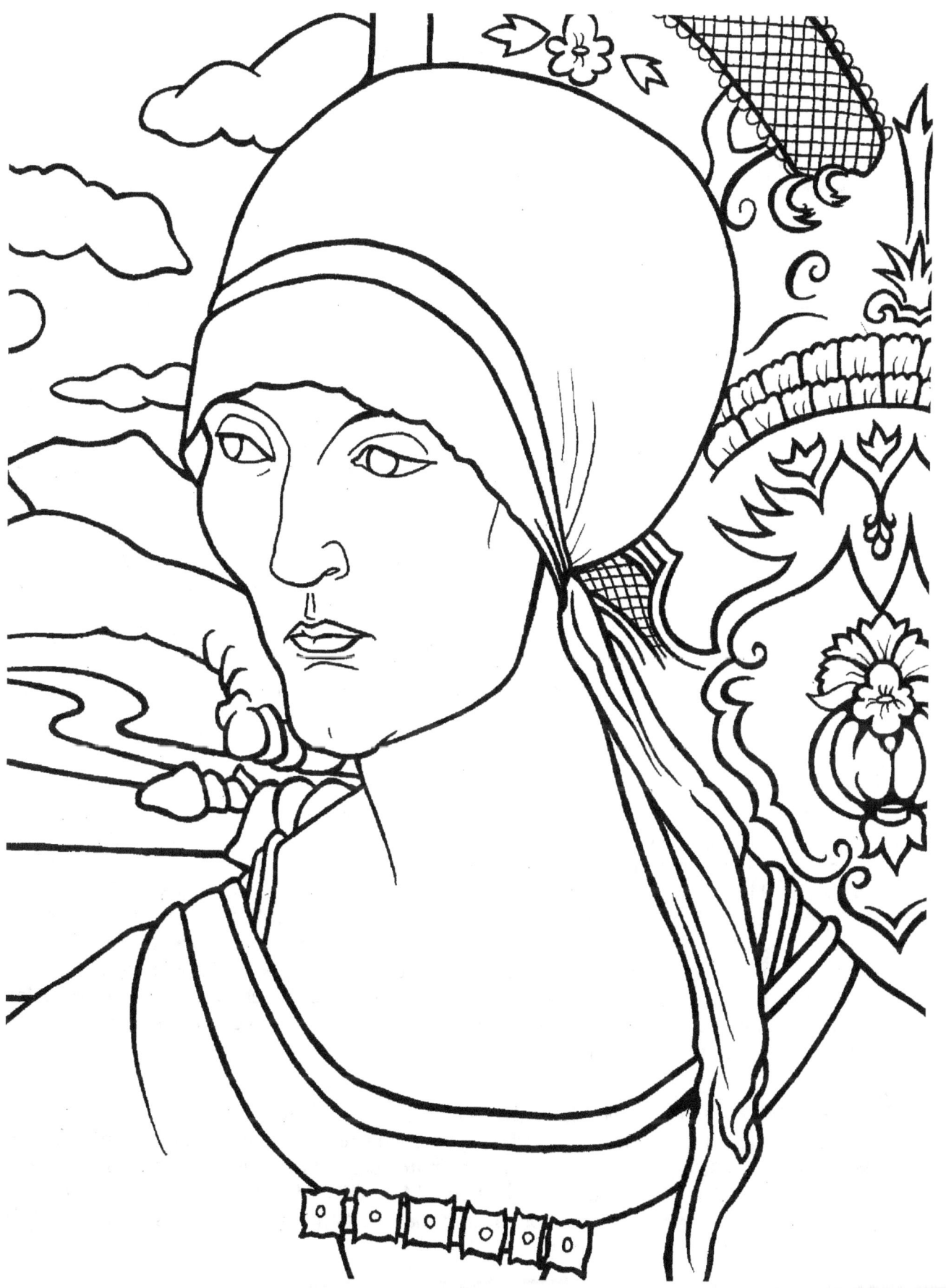

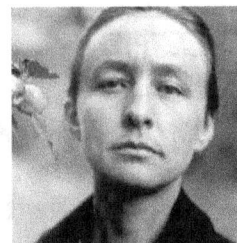

Georgia O'keefe
(November 15, 1887 – March 6, 1986)

🎨 Georgia Totto O'keefe was born in Sun Prairie, Wisconsin on November 15, 1887. Her parents were Francis Calyxtus O'Keeffe and Ida (Totto) O'Keeffe, both dairy farmers. Georgia was the second child born to the O'Keefe's out of seven total.

🎨 At the age of 10, Georgia began receiving art instruction from local watercolor artist, Sara Mann. In 1905, she attended the School of the Art Institute of Chicago. In 1907 she attended the Art Students League in New York City. Her breakthrough in the art world came in 1915 when she sent some charcoal drawings to her friend Anita Pollitzer, who in turn showed them to her friend and gallery owner, Alfred Stieglitz.

🎨 O'Keefe's first art exhibit was held without her knowledge by Alfred Stieglitz at his *291 Gallery*, in 1916. When Georgia found out about the exhibit, she confronted Stieglitz, wanting the paintings to be removed; however, finally relenting, she allowed the exhibit to continue. She made a lasting impression with her flower paintings, done in a very up-close perspective; and with her vivid paintings of the New Mexico landscape. On November 20, 2014, her painting of *Jimson Weed/White Flower No. 1* (the illustration you will be coloring here), sold for $44,405,000!

🎨 Georgia began working with Stieglitz in 1918. The two fell in love very quickly, even though Stieglitz was 23 years her senior and married at the time; though he was trying to get a divorce. His divorce was approved in 1924; Stieglitz and O'Keefe were married four months later. Problems arose in the marriage after a time and Georgia began retreating to Taos, New Mexico. On July 13, 1946, during one of her retreats, Stieglitz died suddenly, having suffering cerebral thrombosis. After settling his estate, Georgia made New Mexico her permanent residence. Though it was a difficult time, this was the most productive period in her career. Many of her most famous paintings were done during this time at her new home, Ghost Ranch, north of Abiquiú. In 1973 a young potter named Juan Hamilton came to her ranch house looking for work. O'Keefe employed the man to work on the ranch, though he eventually became more, as her dearest companion and business manager.

🎨 Around the age of 85, Georgia began to lose her eyesight and could no longer paint. She did, however, continue working on pottery with Juan's help. At the age of 98, on March 6, 1986, Georgia O'Keefe passed away due to natural causes. As was her wish, she was cremated and her ashes scattered from the top of Pedernal Mountain. After her death, there was much discord among the family when they discovered that she had left her entire estate to her dear friend, Juan Hamilton.

Jimson Weed/White Flower No. 1 (1936) by Georgia O'Keefe

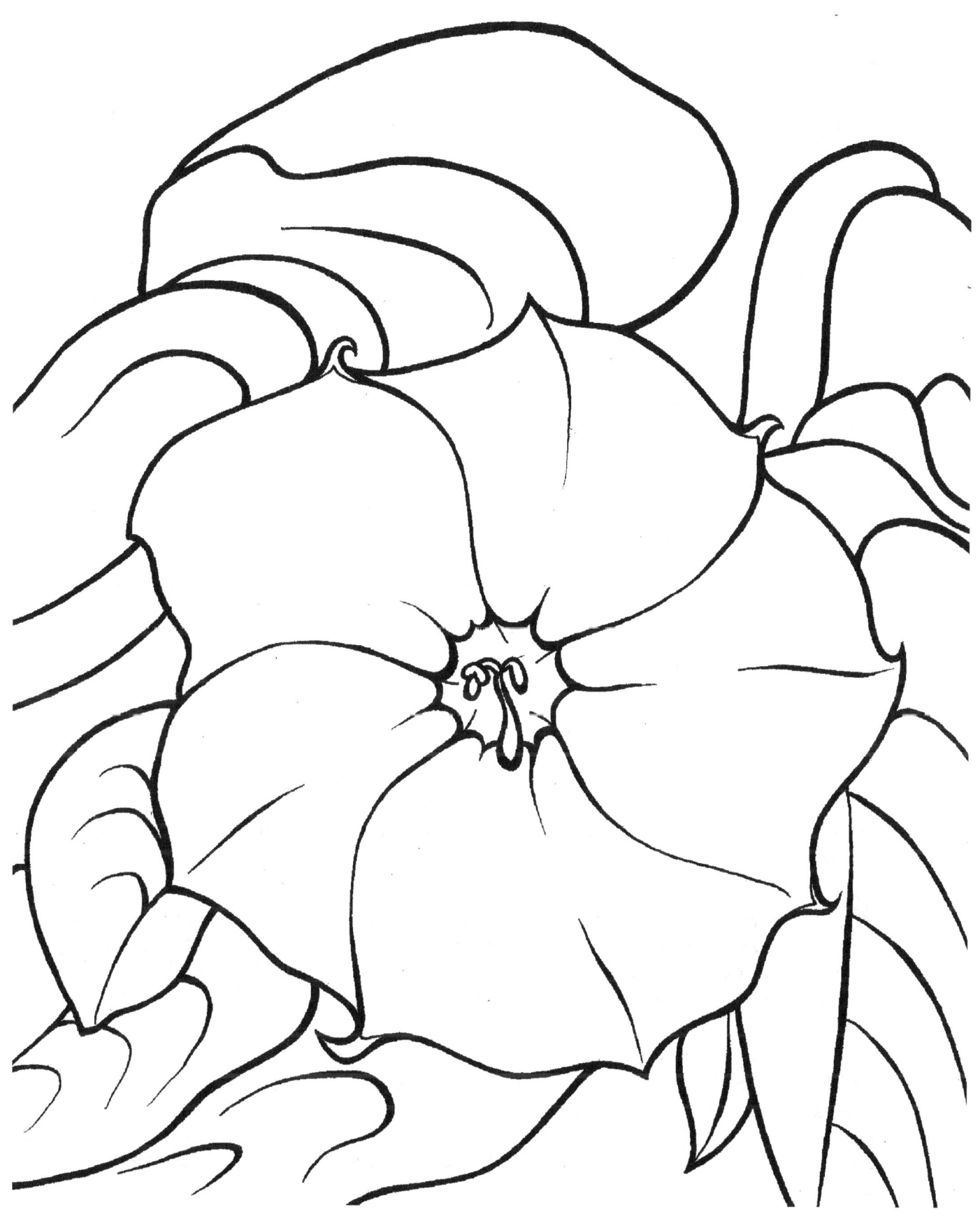

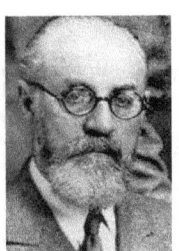

Henri Matisse
(December 31, 1869 – November 3, 1954)

Henri-Émile-Benoît Matisse was born on December 31, 1869 in his grandmother's cottage, at Le Cateau-Cambrésis, in northern France. His father, Émile Hippolyte Matisse, was a grain merchant; his mother, Anna Heloise Gerard, was a hat maker. Henri was one of three sons, although his youngest brother died at the age of two.

In 1887, at the age of 18, Henri began working towards a career in law, following his father's wishes for him. It wasn't until 1889 that he discovered a passion for art. While on bedrest after an attack of appendicitis, Henri was given a gift of art supplies from his mother. She had simply hoped to help him pass the time while he lay abed, but instead she sparked a fire in him and art became his new passion and focus. His father was greatly disappointed when, instead of returning to law school, young Henri enrolled at the Académie Julian to study art in 1891.

In the beginning, Henri painted landscapes, portraits and still life, but his work would greatly evolve and expand over the years to include other forms of art such as printmaking and sculpting. In the early 1900s, Matisse and André Derain would lead a movement in Fauvism; a style of painting that emphasizes "vivid expressionistic and non-naturalistic use of color." [1]

Through his journey in art, he was inspired and influenced by artists such as Nicolas Poussin, Antoine Watteau, Édouard Manet and Jean-Baptiste-Siméon Chardin; also through his friendship with notable artists such as Camille Pissarro and Pablo Picasso. He was first introduced to impressionism when he met John Peter Russell, an Australian painter. Vincent van Gogh's work further impressed young Matisse with this style, which ultimately inspired a change in his own artwork.

In 1894 Henri had one daughter, Marguerite, from a relationship with the model, Caroline Joblau. In 1898 he married Amélie Noellie Parayre. Henri raised his daughter Marguerite together with his new bride, in addition to their own two sons, Jean (born 1899) and Pierre (born 1900). His daughter and wife would often serve as models for his work. The 41-year marriage ended in 1939.

In 1941 Henri Matisse was diagnosed with Duodenal Cancer, located in the lower intestines. The cancer was removed and he survived, but the surgery nearly killed him and he was on bedrest for months. Thirteen years later, at the age of 84, on November 3, 1954, Henri Matisse died of a heart attack. His remains were interred at the cemetery of the Monastère Notre Dame de Cimiez, near Nice.

Madras Rouge (1907) by Henri Matisse

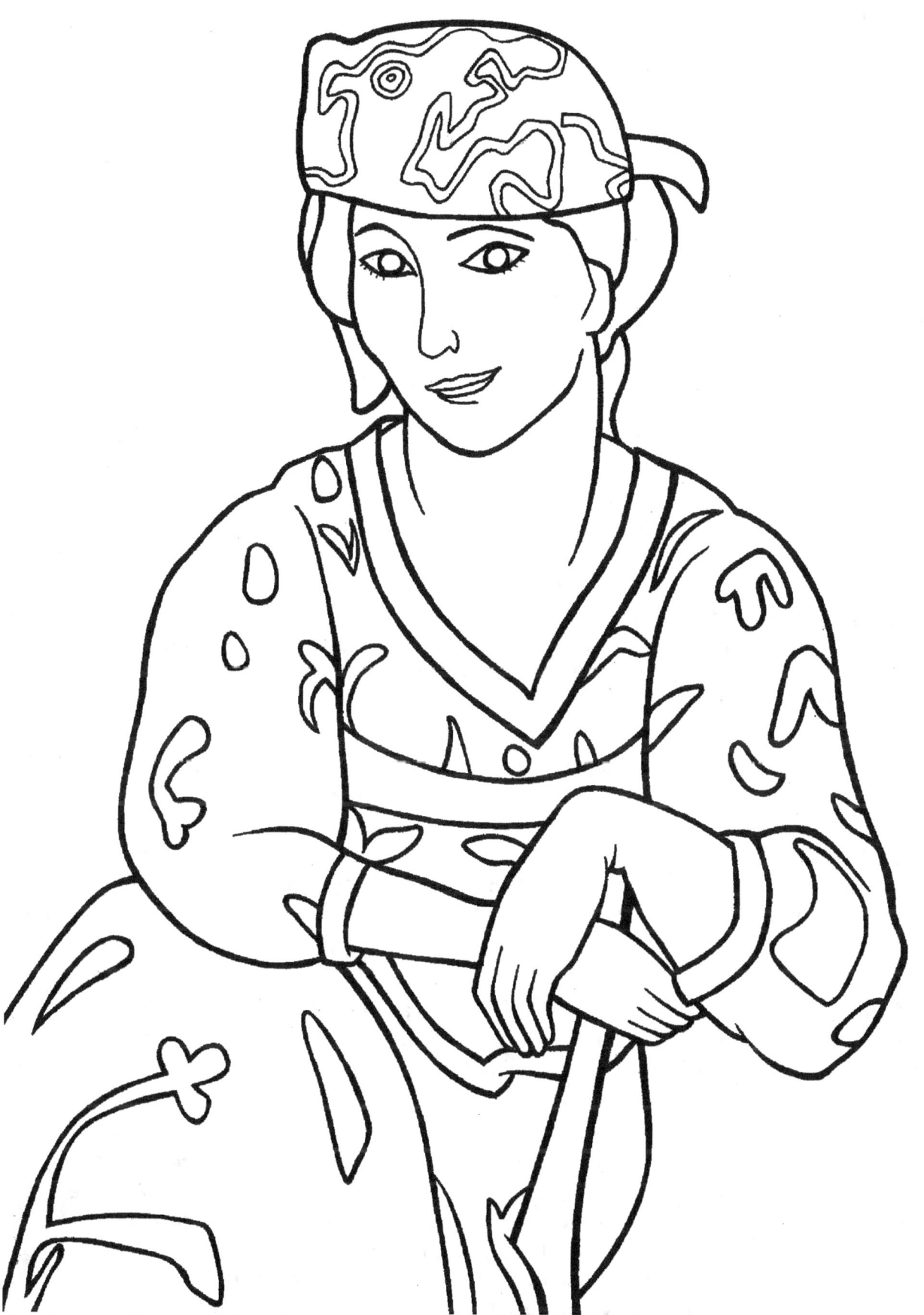

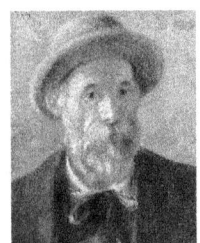

Pierre-Auguste Renoir
(February 25, 1841 – December 3, 1919)

Pierre-Auguste Renoir was born on February 25, 1841, in Limoges, Haute-Vienne, France. His father, Léonard Renoir, was a tailor; and his mother, Marguerite Merlet, was a dressmaker. Pierre was the sixth of their seven children.

Renoir had his first experience in art around 1844, as he worked in a porcelain factory, painting plates. In 1862, he would move on to formally study painting with Charles Gleyre, in Paris. Renoir's career as an artist was a struggle in the beginning; the Salon de Paris rejected his work and often he could not even afford to buy paint.

Rebelling against the tradition of painting historical and religious scenes in darker tones, Renoir and several other young artists ventured out into society to paint bright, vividly colored landscapes, active with people. Their newly developing technique, later called *Impressionism,* would focus on capturing the light, colors in shadow, texture in brush strokes and the vibrant energy of each real-life scene. It was a beautiful, innovative style, though it would not be accepted by the critics of their time, who preferred realism and the more muted, traditional tones.

Being turned down by the Salon de Paris, Renoir and his fellow Impressionists protested the rejection until finally the Emperor, Napoleon III agreed that the shunned art could be displayed elsewhere for the public to form their own opinions, outside of the Salon. And so, the Salon de Refusés (The exhibit of rejects) was opened in 1874. With this exhibit, they did find a few strong supporters and the Impressionist movement slowly came to rise in the eye of the art world. Renoir, Monet, Manet, Pissarro and Cézanne would be some of the leading figures in this artistic revolution.

In 1885 Renoir had a son, Pierre Renoir (the actor), with Aline Victorine Charigot. In 1890, the couple married and had two more sons; Jean Renoir (the filmmaker) and Claude Renoir (a ceramic artist). His wife and children would appear as subjects in many of the artist's paintings.

Around 1892 Renoir developed rheumatoid arthritis, which limited his abilities in painting, but did not stop him entirely. In 1912, he suffered a stroke that would leave him in a wheelchair— yet, he continued to paint and to sculpt. He would keep painting for the remaining 20 years of his life. Renoir lived just long enough to see one of his works bought by the *Louvre* in 1919. He died of heart failure on the third day of that December (1919), at the age of 78, in his home. He was respectfully interred in Essoyes Cimetière, France.

A Girl (1885) by Pierre-Auguste Renoir

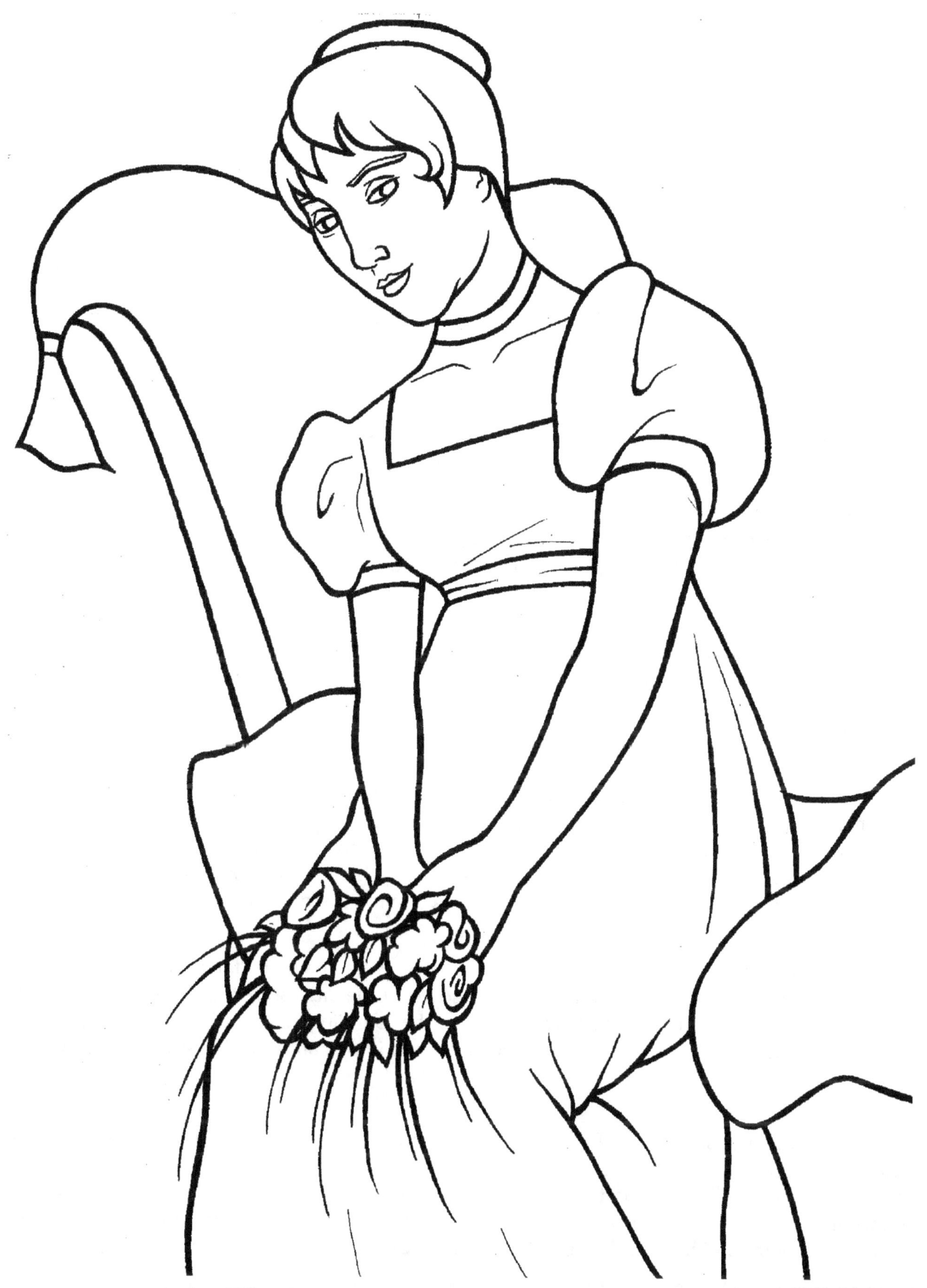

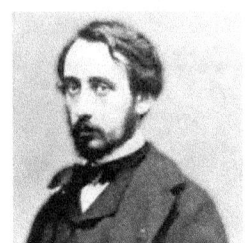

Edgar Degas
(July 19, 1834 –September 27, 1917)

Hilaire-Germain-Edgar Degas was born in Paris, France on July 19, 1834. His father, Augustin De Gas, was a French banker; His mother, Célestine Musson De Gas, was an American from New Orleans. Edgar was the oldest of their five children. For a time, the Degas family presented their name as "de Gas", but Edgar would later choose to use the more modest spelling of the name, Degas.

Degas displayed a talent for art at a very young age and was greatly encouraged by his father, who was an avid art lover. By the age of 18, he received permission to visit the Louvre in Paris where he would copy the work of the masters. This was a common practice for aspiring artists of his time; copying/making a study by replicating the techniques of master artists. Around the age of 21, Edgar would attend the École des Beaux-Arts in Paris, but only for one year. He left the school to travel Italy, eager to explore and study more techniques from other artists.

In 1862, at the age of 28, Degas met a fellow painter named Edouard Manet. The two artists shared in their disapproval of the limits set upon artists by the current establishments; those preferring traditional styles of painting and rejecting modern exploration of art. Degas and Manet quickly developed a friendly rivalry as they both explored the techniques of Impressionism, under heavy public criticism.

To overcome the oppression of traditional art expectations and limits, Degas and several other painters formed the Société Anonyme des Artistes (Society of Independent Artists). The group held their own exhibitions after their work had been rejected as inappropriate and too modern. Degas' paintings were of the Impressionistic style and were often of dancers or nude women, which had not been acceptable unless it was a biblical depiction.

Degas never married, nor did he have children, as he chose to devote his entire life and focus to art. He did not have any formal pupils; however, he did inspire many other artists during and after his life. He came to be known as one of the founding fathers of Impressionism. Degas was one of the rare few who would see the effect and importance of his creative works within his own lifetime.

In the later years of his life, Degas' eyesight began to fail. He struggled through the growing disability, painting up until 1912, when he was finally forced to quit. Art had been everything to him throughout his life, his truest love. The loss of this lifelong 'companion' led him into a deep depression and reclusive behavior for the remaining years of his life. On September 27, 1917 Degas died of unspecified causes. He is buried in the Cimitière de Montmartre of Paris, France.

Music Hall Singer (La Chanson du Chien) (c. 1875-77) by Edgar Degas

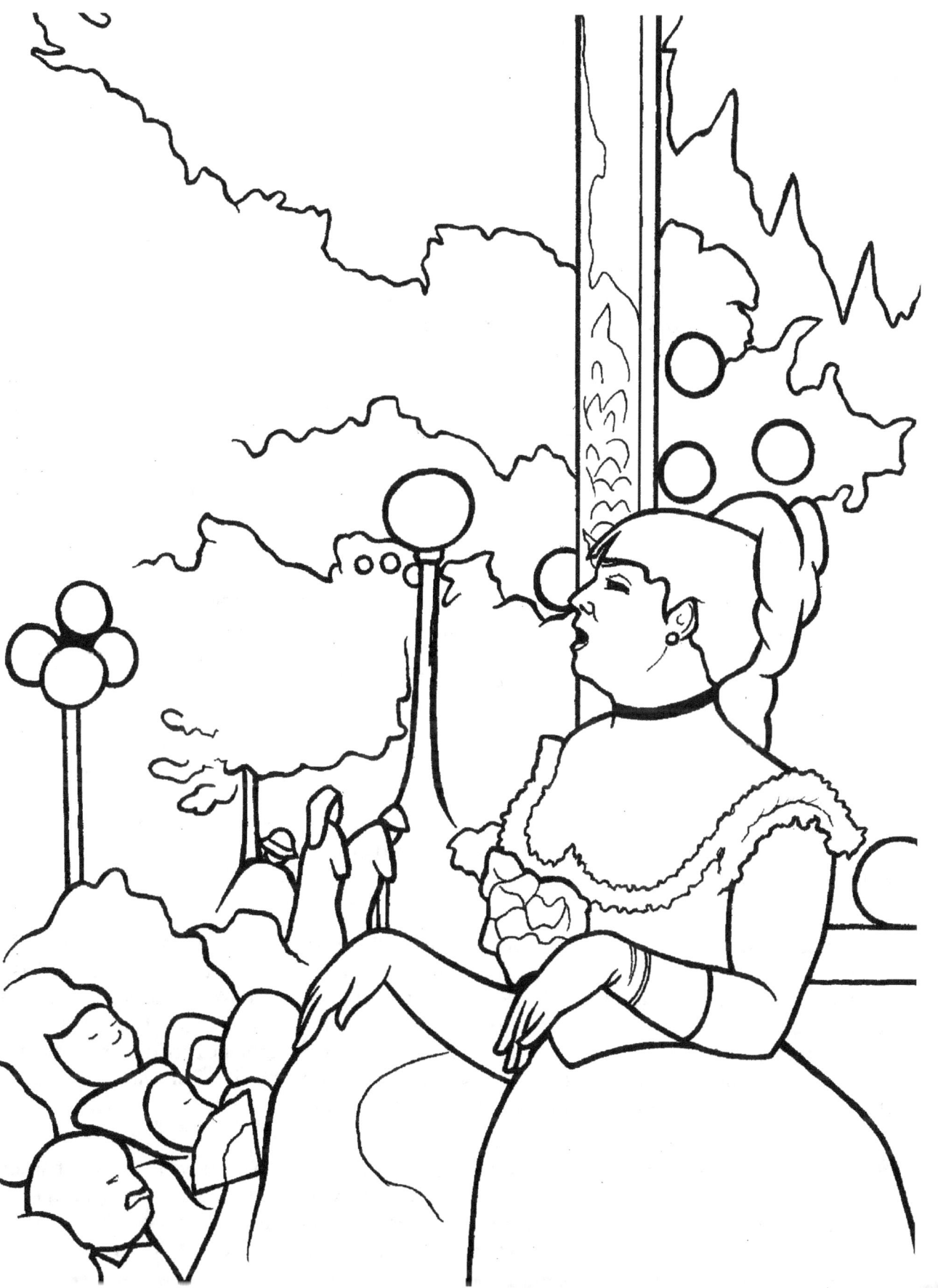

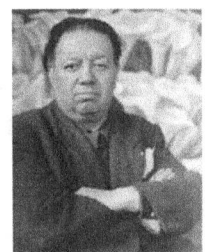

Diego Rivera
(December 8, 1886 – November 24, 1957)

Diego Rivera was born on December 8, 1886, in Guanajuato, Mexico. His parents were Diego Rivera Acosta and María del Pilar Barrientos. His siblings were María del Pilar and Carlos Rivera Barrientos (Diego's twin brother who died two years after their birth).

Diego's love of art began as a child, around one year after his twin brother passed away. One story goes that, when he was caught drawing on the walls of his home, instead of punishing their son, his parents encouraged his creativity by installing chalk boards on the walls. When Diego was about 10 years old, he attended the San Carlos Academy of Fine Arts, in Mexico City. When he was 21, he took this passion further and continued his education abroad as he traveled to Europe to study the masters.

Diego's passion for art was mingled with his passion for the people of Mexico. From the very beginning, his creative muse was the people of his country; their joys, their hardships, the reality of Mexican society. He was very well known in his lifetime for the illustrations of his people, as well as for the very political content in his murals.

In 1921, Rivera was part of a government program which funded his work on a series of public murals. Rivera was very outspoken in his political standings and he often portrayed this in his work, making many of his paintings very controversial. In his fresco of the *Man at the Crossroads*, in New York City's RCA building, there was a portrait of Vladimir Lenin; because of this inclusion, the mural was cancelled and destroyed by the Rockefeller family, after Diego refused to alter his vision.

In total, Diego would marry 4 women in his lifetime; Angeline Beloff (1909 – 1921), Guadalupe Marín ('Lupe', 1922 - 1927), Frida Kahlo (m. 1929 – div. 1938 and remarried m. 1940 – 1954), and Emma Hurtado (m. 1955 – 1957). His most notable marriage was to the artist, Frida Khalo. Diego and Frida had no children together, though she became pregnant multiple times. The couple suffered many miscarriages, due to Frida's injuries from the bus accident that she had suffered as a young woman. Diego did however have a son with his first wife, Angeline; a daughter with one of his extramarital affairs; and two daughters with his second wife, Lupe.

In 1955 Diego Rivera was diagnosed with cancer. This was the same year that he married Emma Hurtado, his art dealer. Diego would have a surgery and fully recover from the cancer, only to die two years later, in 1957, from a heart attack in his studio. Upon his death, Diego willed all his art to the Mexican Nation. He is buried at the Panteón Civil de Dólores, in Mexico City, Mexico.

The Flower Vendor (1935) By Diego Rivera

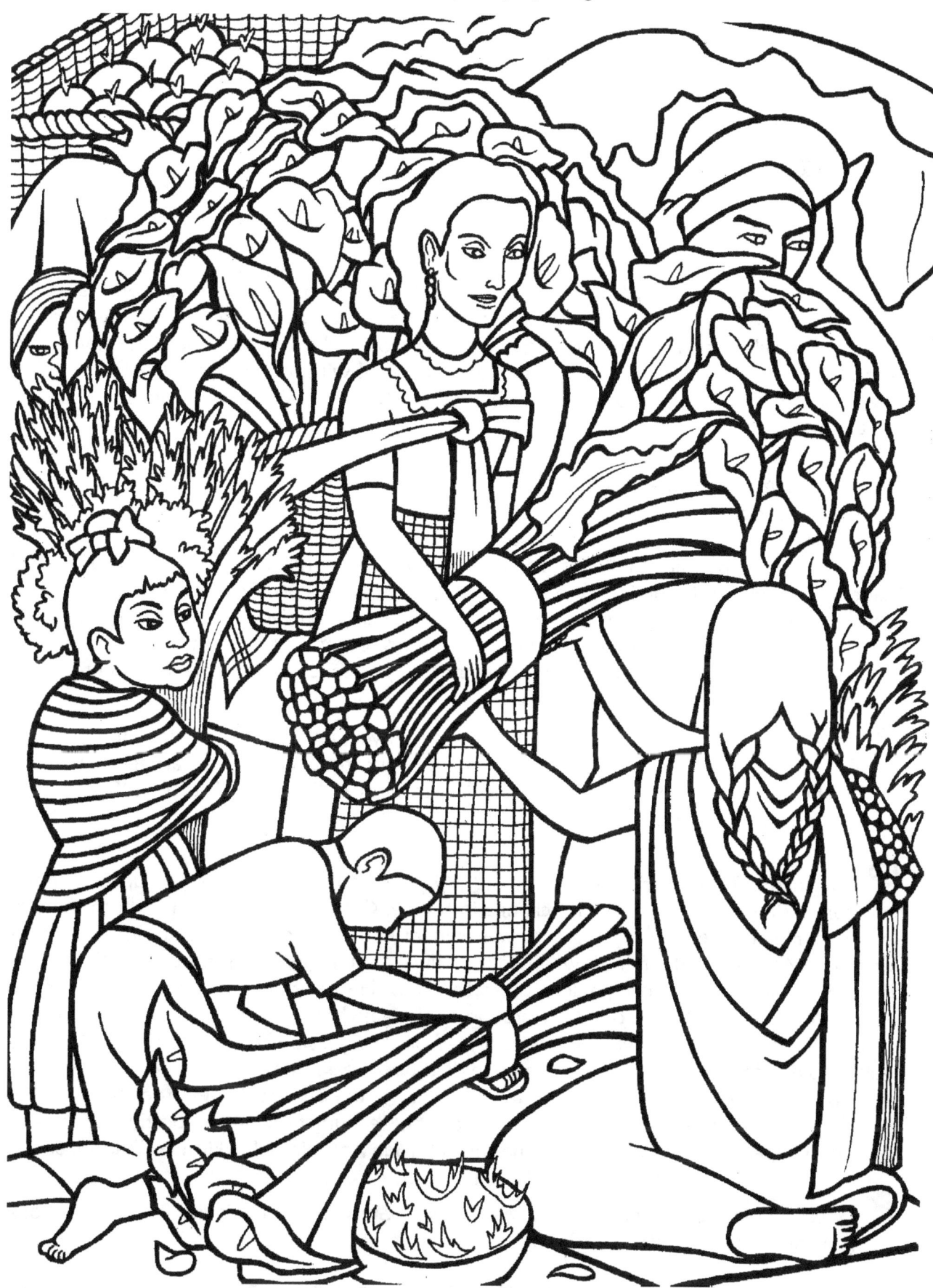

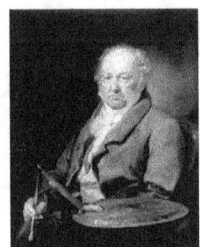

Francisco Goya
(March 30, 1746 – April 16, 1828)

🎨 Francisco José de Goya y Lucientes was born in Fuendetodos, Aragón, Spain, on March 30, 1746. His parents were José Benito de Goya y Franque and Gracia de Lucientes y Salvador. His father was a gilder of religious objects; an artist who works with *gold leaf* or powder to decoratively cover surfaces such as wood, stone, or metal with a thin layer of gold. Francisco was the fourth child born out of a total of six children; Rita, Tomás, Jacinta, Francisco, Mariano and Camilo.

🎨 Goya began his formal studies in art at the age of 14 when he became a student of the painter José Luzán. Under Luzán's tutelage, Goya learned to copy stamps and would do this for a few years before going to work on his own. He also studied in Madrid, with Anton Raphael Mengs, who was a popular painter for Spanish royalty. After being denied entrance into the Real Academia de Bellas Artes de San Fernando, both in 1763 and 1766, Goya traveled to Rome to pursue his studies in art. After his return to Aragon, Francisco studied with the Aragónese artist, Francisco Bayeu y Subías. During this time, Goya's work began to evolve into the style that he would be famous for as he became one of the most important Spanish painters of his time.

🎨 Goya became friends with his teacher, Francisco Bayeu, and married his sister Josefa Bayeu on July 25, 1773. They would have many pregnancies and equally many miscarriages. Only one of their children would make it to adulthood, their son, Javier Goya. Josefa died in 1812, leaving Goya to raise the boy alone.

🎨 Goya had suffered a serious illness around 1793 that had left him completely deaf. With this handicap, a dramatic and unpleasant change in his life, Goya was a broken man both in body and mind. He became very depressed, as was evident in the darker more pessimistic tone of his later work. Around 1824, after his wife had long since died, he left Spain to retire in the French city of Bordeaux, with his companion, Leocadia Weiss. His health continued to fail him as the years went on; first with the slow deterioration of his eyesight and then finally when he suffered a stroke. With the stroke, Goya was left paralyzed on his right side and in a comatose state. His health rapidly declined from this point and he died two weeks later, on April 16 of 1828 at the age of 82. Goya was originally buried at the Cemetery of the Chartreuse of Bordeaux. Later, the Spanish government requested and was granted the exhumation and relocation of Goya's remains to a grave beneath the floor of the church in San Antonio del la Florida, Madrid, Spain.

🎨 Goya is portrayed in the 2006 movie, "Goya's Ghost"; starring Javier Bardem, Natalie Portman and Stellan Skarsgård (as Goya).

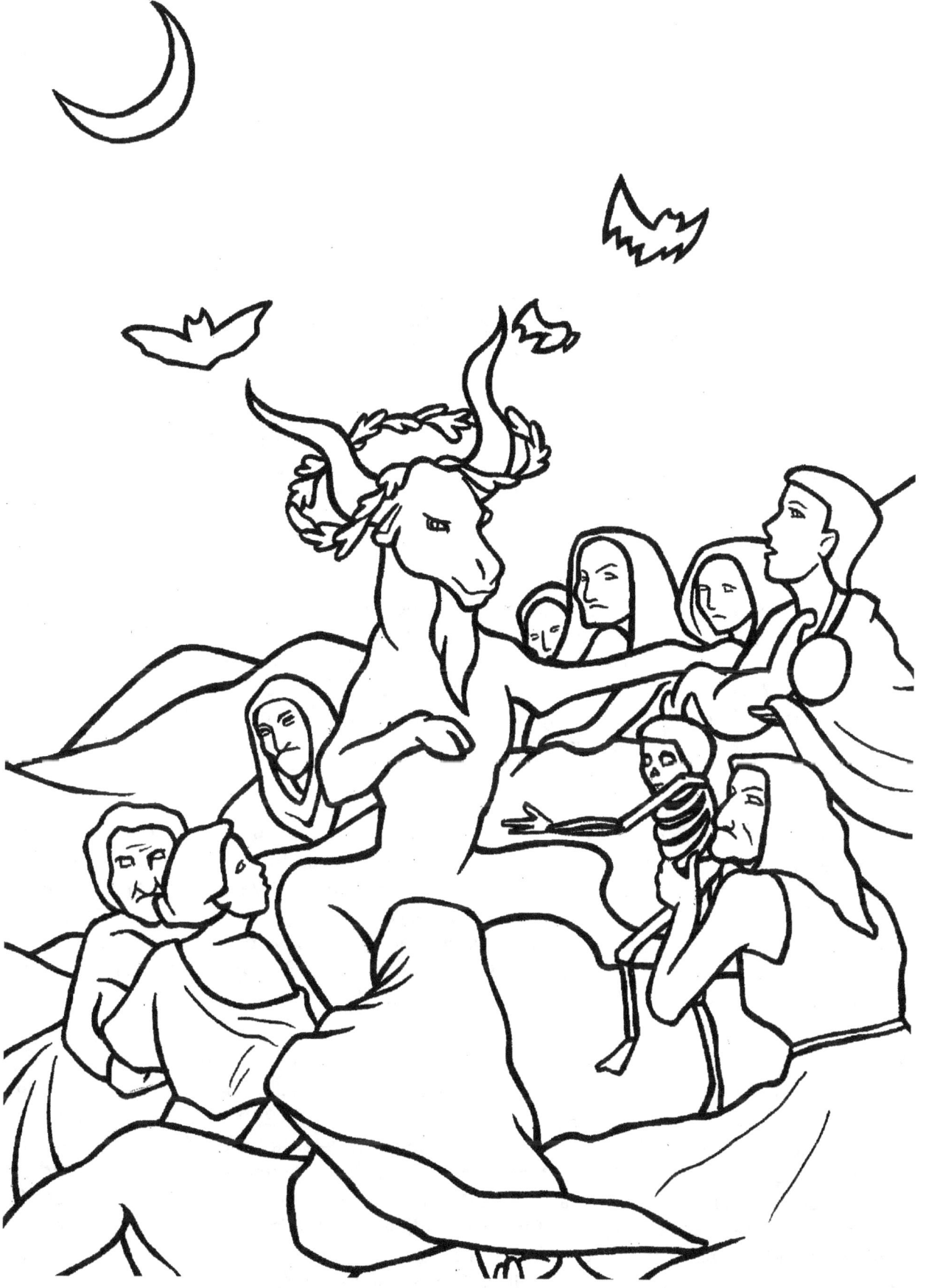

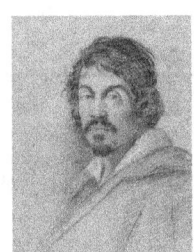

Caravaggio
(September 29, 1571 – July 18, 1610)

Michelangelo Merisi da Caravaggio was born on September 29, 1571 in Milan, Italy. He is most commonly known as Caravaggio, though this is *not* his name-- rather it is the name of where he lived; Michelangelo Merisi da (of) Caravaggio. His mother was Lucia Aratori and his father was Fermo Merisi, the architect to the Marchese de Caravaggio.

In 1584, the same year that his mother died, Caravaggio would begin a 4-year apprenticeship with Simone Peterzano, a Milanese painter and pupil of Titian's. In 1592 he fled to Rome after injuring a police officer in a quarrel—he was a notorious brawler. In Rome, he would work for Guiseppe Cesari in a painting workshop. Caravaggio was eventually discovered when he attracted the patronage of, Cardinal Francesco Maria del Monte, one of the leading art connoisseurs of Rome.

Caravaggio was famous within his own lifetime—known for the striking realism of his paintings. He didn't idealize his subjects, as was the traditional method of the time; rather, he preferred to portray his subjects just as they were—bitter flaws and all. He was quite a novelty in his time, received with a mix of both admirers and harsh critics. Some saw his realism as miraculous talent, while others deemed it as vulgar. This talent attracted many private commissions, as well as for the public in places such as the Contarelli Chapel in the Church of San Luigi dei Francesi.

Many of Caravaggio's commissioned works were rejected by the intended buyers and he had to repaint them or find someone else to buy them. While his intense realism was often appreciated, sometimes it was just too much for the more conservative people. For his *Groom's Madonna* painting, which was removed from view, a cardinal's secretary wrote: "In this painting there are but vulgarity, sacrilege, impiousness and disgust...One would say it is a work made by a painter that can paint well, but of a dark spirit, and who has been for a lot of time far from God, from His adoration, and from any good thought..."[1]

Caravaggio's life was a mix of fame and defame, as he rose high in the art world but cast himself down in the social realm with his tendencies for brawling. His police records were enough to fill numerous pages. The worst of his actions happened on the 29th of May, 1606, when he killed a young man named Ranuccio Tomassoni. The exact details of the fight and of the death remain unknown, though it is said that it may have been accidental. After the incident, Caravaggio fled to Naples as an outlaw. In 1610, Caravaggio travelled to the Pope in hopes of a pardon. What happened after his departure, and leading up to his death on July 18th, is unknown. It was reported that he died of a fever, but some speculate that he was murdered. Michelangelo Merisi da Caravaggio is buried at the Cimitero San Sebastiano, Tuscany, Italy.

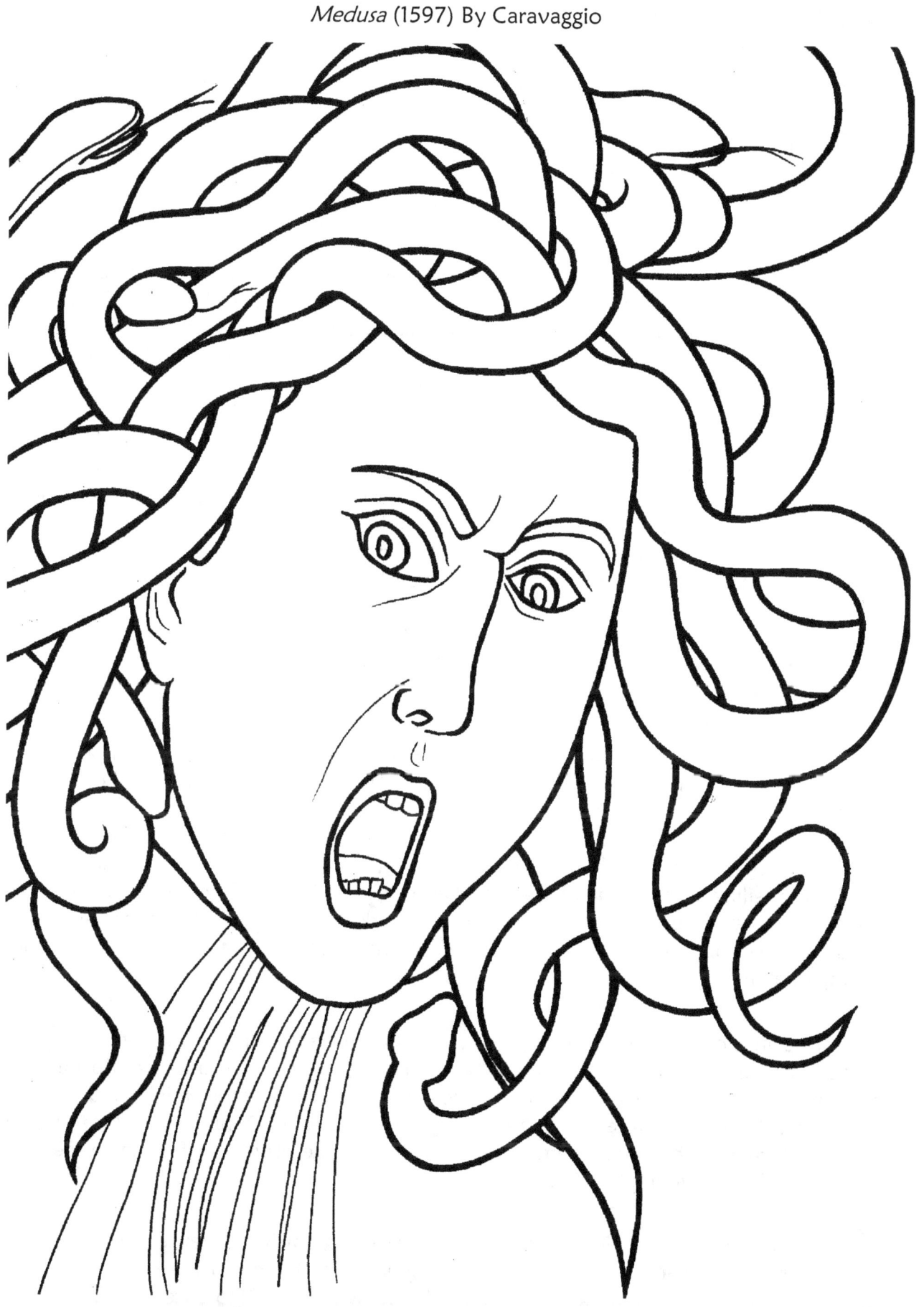

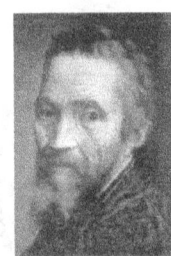

Michelangelo di Lodovico
(March 6, 1475 – February 18, 1564)

Michelangelo di Lodovico Buonarroti Simoni was born on March 6, 1475 in Caprese; a village in the province of Arezzo, Tuscany, Italy. His father, Ludovico di Leonardo Buonarroti Simoni, was the Judicial administrator of the village. His mother, Francesca di Neri del Miniato di Siena, died when Michelangelo was only six years old. Michelangelo had 4 siblings; Buonarroto, Leonardo, Giovan and Gismondo

After his mother's death, Michelangelo most often stayed with his nanny and her husband, who was a stonecutter. This exposure would be the seed of creativity that led the young boy into his love for marble. Michelangelo's father soon realized that his son had a passion and talent for art and, when he was 13, his father arranged for an apprenticeship with Ghirlandaio. Within a year, Ghirlandaio received a request from Lorenzo de' Medici, to whom he sent Michelangelo as one of his best pupils.

Gaining a reputation through his work for the Medici family, Michelangelo's talents became much sought after in the religious society. He was commissioned to do work for great leaders such as Pope Clement VII, Pope Julius II and Pope Leo X.

In 1505, Michelangelo was commissioned to build a magnificent tomb for Pope Julius II, located in the Church of San Pietro in Vincoli, Rome. Attaining this commission caused much envy from a fellow artist, Bramante. According to Condivi's account, the rival artist spitefully convinced the pope to commission Michelangelo in a medium that was less familiar to him, in hopes that he would fail and lose favor ([1]). Michelangelo was thus commissioned to paint the ceiling of the Sistine Chapel—and as we all know, he did *not* fail in this task, but rose even higher in the world of art. The finished work stretches over 500 square meters of the chapel's ceiling, containing over 300 figures and is one of the artist's most notable accomplishments.

Michelangelo was a very solitary man, devoting his entire life to the arts. He never married and had no children, but he did bring many great things into this world through sculpture, painting, architecture and poetry. He was a vessel of endless creativity and talent—deemed the "father and master of all the arts" ([2]). He was one of the rare few artists to know fame and fortune in his own lifetime, as well as having the privilege of living to see two publications for the biography of his life.

In 1564, Michelangelo died in Rome at the blessed age of 88. His exact cause of death is unknown, but he had been ill with a fever. He was laid to rest in the Basilica of Santa Croce; as his final wish was to be laid to rest in his beloved city of Florence.

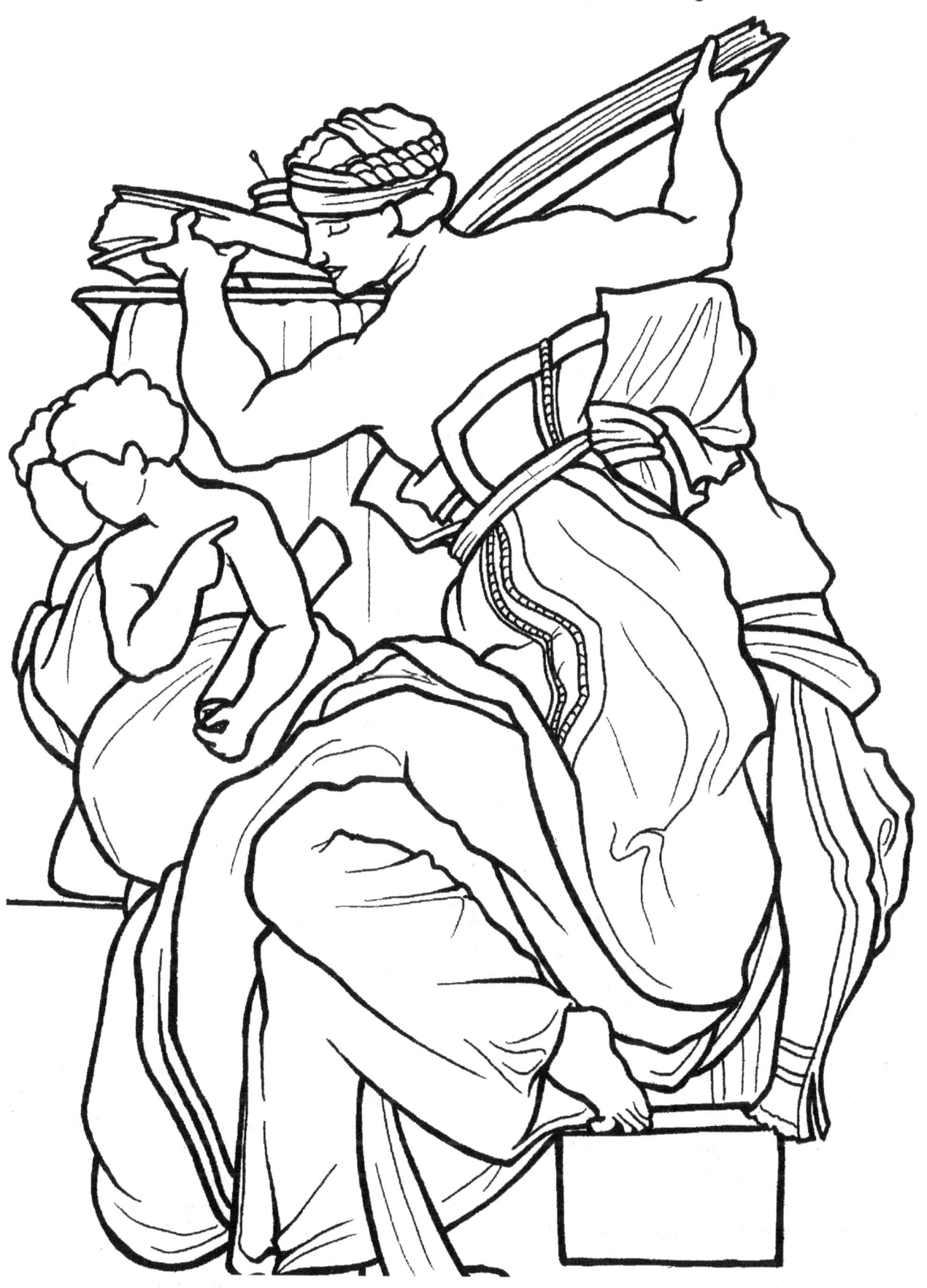

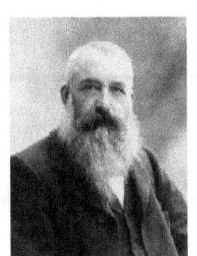

Claude Monet
(November 14, 1840 – December 5, 1926)

🎨 Oscar-Claude Monet was born on November 14th, 1840 in Paris, France. His parents were Claude Adolphe Monet and Louise Justine Aubrée Monet. He had one older brother named Leon. His mother died in 1857, when Monet was seventeen.

🎨 Monet began charcoal drawing lessons with the French artist, Jacques-François Ochard. Later he met Eugène Boudin, a French landscape artist who would become Monet's mentor in oil painting. With Boudin, he would be introduced to the beautiful art of painting landscape outdoors, *en plein-air*. He later became a student of Charles Gleyre, in Paris, where he met the artists Édouard Manet and Pierre-Auguste Renoir.

🎨 Monet was one of the founding fathers for Impressionism. He applied this technique to his work, focusing on the landscape around him. Often he would paint the same outdoor scene over and over, capturing the different phases of daylight, passing seasons and weather in one location. For example; he spent around 20 years painting and repainting the water lilies on his property in Giverny, France.

🎨 Monet and his fellow impressionist artists were rejected by the *Académie des Beaux-Art's* annual exhibition at the *Salon de Paris*, but they didn't give up on their dream. In 1873, Monet, Camille Pissarro, Pierre-Auguste Renoir and Alfred Sisley organized their own Société Anonyme des Artistes Peintres, Sculpteurs et Graveurs (Anonymous Society of Painters, Sculptors, and Engravers). It was through this society that they would exhibit their art independently and where Monet would exhibit his painting, *Soleil Levant* (*Impression*, Sunrise), which gave the group its signature name.

🎨 *The Woman in the Green Dress* was one of the many paintings where Monet would use Camille Doncieux as his model; the woman who would later become his wife. They had their first child, Jean, in 1867. Monet and Camille were later married on June 28, 1870. They would have another son in 1878, named Michel Monet.

🎨 The later years of Monet's life were filled with much sorrow. In 1876 his wife became ill and then was diagnosed with uterine cancer. They had a small measure of joy when their second son, Michel, was born in early 1878, but the birth further weakened Camille's fragile health and she died on the September 5th, 1879. It was a very difficult time for Monet, but from this period of grief came some of his best paintings. The widowed Monet was left with two sons to care for; his friend's wife, Alice Hoschedé, was in a similar situation and so the two decided to help one another. Monet later married Alice Hoschedé in 1892. Alice died in 1911; Monet died of lung cancer fifteen years later, on December 5th, 1926 at the age of 86. He is buried in the Giverny Church Cemetery. His home, with the famed water lily pond, is open for touring in Giverny, France.

The Walk, Woman with a Parasol (1875) By Monet

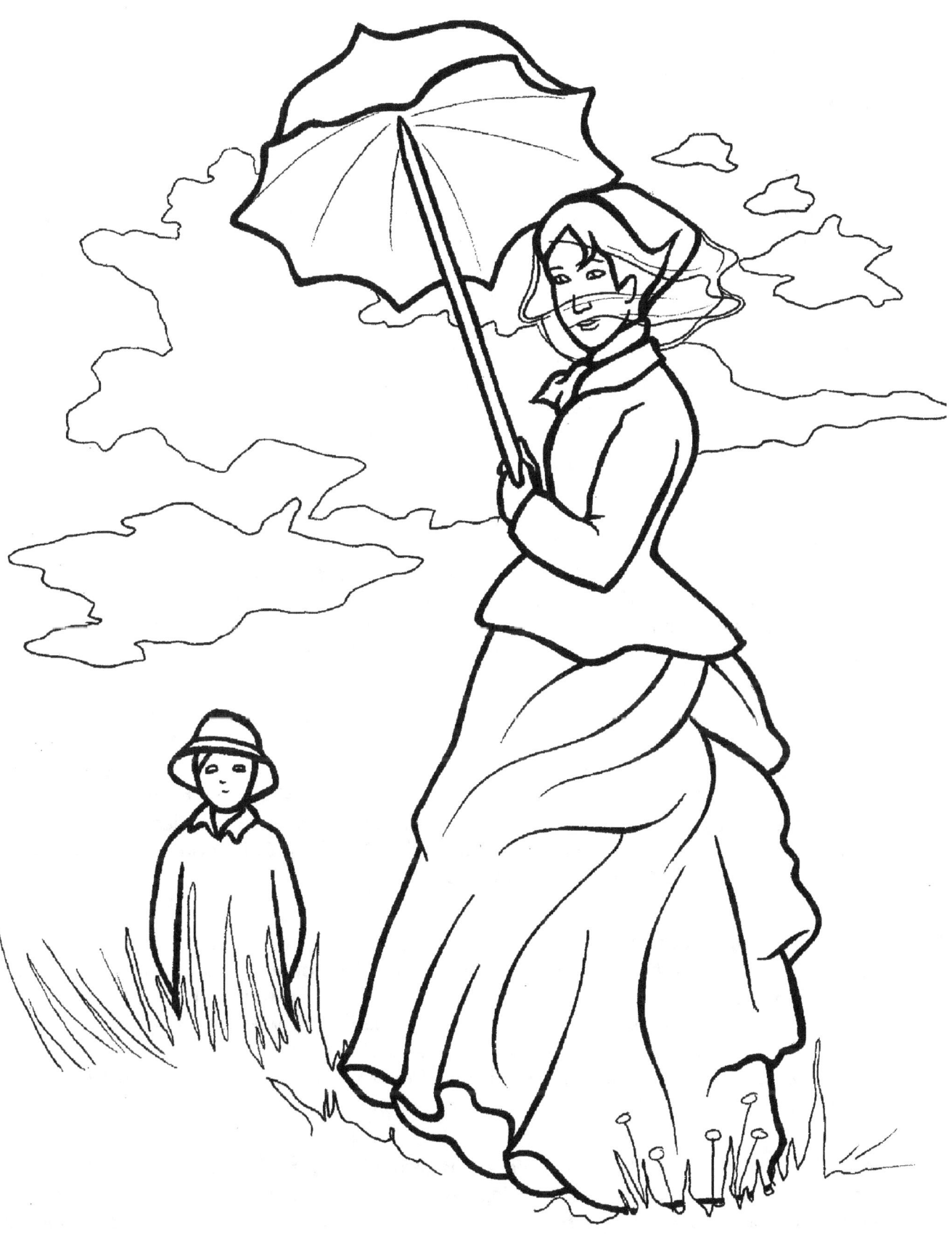

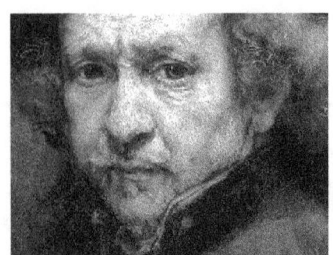

Rembrandt van Rijn
(July 15, 1606 – October 4, 1669)

🎨 Rembrandt Harmenszoon van Rijn was born on July 15, 1606 in Leiden, a city and municipality of the Dutch province of South Holland. His parents were Harmen Gerritszoon van Rijn and Neeltgen Willemsdochter van Zuijtbrouck. His father was a miller and his mother was a baker's daughter. He had around nine, or more, siblings.

🎨 Rembrandt attended Leiden University in 1620, but left soon after to pursue his passion for painting. He began a three-year apprenticeship with the historical painter, Jacob van Swanenburgh. Later, in 1624, he went to Amsterdam and began working with Pieter Lastman, who was a painter of biblical and historical scenes. By 1625, at the age of nineteen, the young artist was working independently and opened his own studio with his friend and fellow student, Jan Lievens.

🎨 Not long after opening his studio, Rembrandt was discovered by an important statesman, Constantijn Huygens, who gave Rembrandt very important commissions from the court of The Hague. This connection continued with Prince Frederik Hendrik continually purchasing paintings for the next 20 years. Rembrandt attained popularity for his portrait paintings and then later for his biblical scenes; becoming one of the greatest Dutch painters and printmakers in art history.

🎨 The most notable collections of Rembrandt's work are at Amsterdam's Rijksmuseum, the Mauritshuis in The Hague, the Hermitage Museum in St. Petersburg, the *National Gallery* in London, Gemäldegalerie in Berlin, Gemäldegalerie Alte Meister in Dresden, The Louvre, The National Museum of Fine Arts in Stockholm, and Schloss Wilhelmshöhe in Kassel. Two of his paintings are displayed at the Royal Castle in Warsaw, and there are also collections of his work in America, kept at the Metropolitan Museum of Art, The Frick Collection in New York City, and in the National Gallery of Art in Washington, D.C.

🎨 In 1634 Rembrandt married Saskia van Uylenburgh. In 1639 the couple moved into a house, which is now known as the Rembrandt House Museum. The couple had a total of four children, only one of which surviving into adulthood; Titus. Sadly, Saskia died in 1642 soon after his birth, most likely from tuberculosis. Rembrandt later had a relationship with Hendrickje Stoffels, and a daughter by her in 1654; Cornelia. The couple was considered legally wed under common law, but they never officially married. Hendrickje died in 1663, leaving Rembrandt with their 9-year-old daughter.

🎨 Rembrandt died on October 4, 1669 in Amsterdam, one year after his son, Titus, had passed away. He was buried as a poor man, having always lived beyond his means. This meant that he was laid to rest in a grave that was loaned by the church. After 20 years, as was customary of "loaned" graves, his remains were exhumed and destroyed.

Flora (1635) By Rembrandt van Rijn

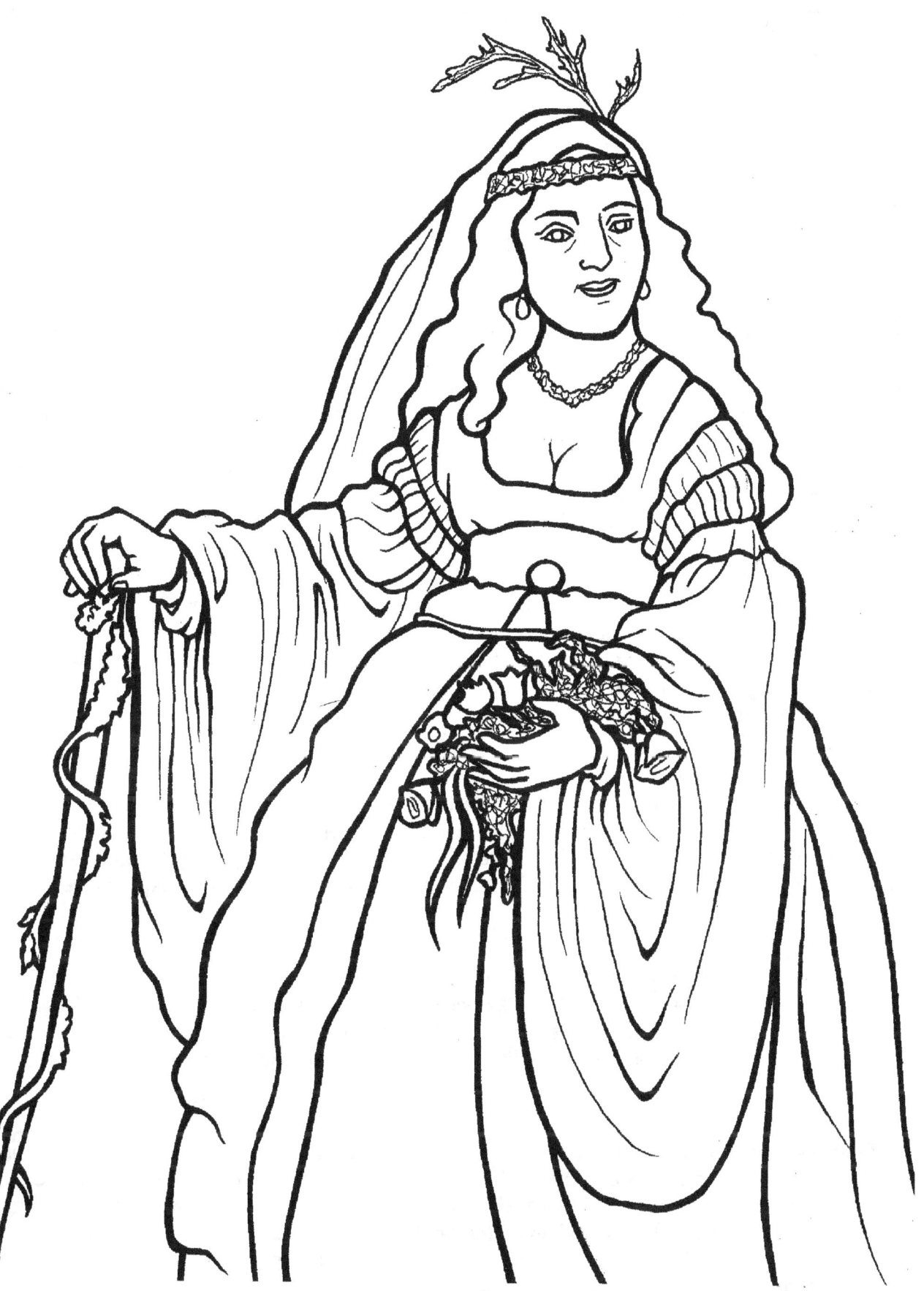

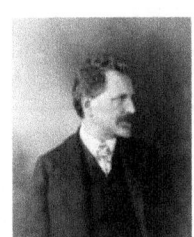

Alphonse Mucha
(July 24, 1860 – July 14, 1939)

Alphonse Maria Mucha was born on July 24, 1860 in Ivančice, Moravia of the Czech Republic. His parents were Ondřej Mucha and Amálie Muchová. He had two sisters, Anna Kuberová and Anděla Muchová (Remundová).

Mucha began his primary education at Saint-Peter's Cathedral in Brno, Moravia. It was here, surrounded by a bounty of Baroque art, that Mucha's creativity was sparked. He began by drawing as a young boy and later moved on to painting. While working as a painter of decorative scenes, Count Karl Khuen discovered and hired Mucha to embellish Hrušovany Emmahof Castle with murals. He was so impressed by Mucha's work, that he decided to fund his formal training at the Munich Academy of Fine Arts. In 1887 the young artist continued his studies at the Académies Julian and Colarossi. In late 1894, Mucha stumbled upon a great opportunity when he created the advertising poster for a play featuring Sarah Bernhardt, a Paris actress; the project led to a six-year contract.

Mucha is well known for his paintings, posters, postcards, advertisements, book illustrations, jewelry designs, carpet and wallpaper designs in a style known as *Art Nouveau* (French for "New Art"). The focus of his art was most often beautiful, young women surrounded by flowers and wearing flowing dresses. He liked to use soft, pastel colors in his work, which was very different from the typical poster artistry.

Mucha considered his painting, *The Slav Epic* (Slovanská epopej), to be the finest art masterpiece of his lifetime. This series consisted of twenty large paintings that illustrated the history and mythology of the Czech and other Slavic people. Mucha himself bestowed this artwork upon the city of Prague in 1928, where the artwork was displayed in Moravský Krumlov for nearly 50 years. After much dispute, the artwork was later moved to the National Gallery's Veletržní Palace, Prague in 2012.

Mucha was married to Maruška (Marie) Chytilová on June 10, 1906, in Prague. During a visit to the U.S. from 1906 to 1910, Maruška became pregnant and gave birth to their daughter, Jaroslava, in New York City. After returning to Prague, they also had a son, Jiří, born in 1915. Jiří would carry on his father's legacy, authoring numerous autobiographies about his father and the artwork that he had created.

In the late 1930s, fascism was a powerful force sweeping through the land, resulting in Mucha being targeted for his artwork and for his Slavic nationalism. When the German troops came to Czechoslovakia in 1939, Mucha was arrested by the Gestapo. During his imprisonment, he became sick with pneumonia and, even though he was released, the illness had taken its toll. Alphonse Mucha died later that same year on July 14, 1939 in Prague. The cause of death was a lung infection. He is buried in the Vyšehrad Cemetery.

Primrose (1899) By Alphonse Mucha

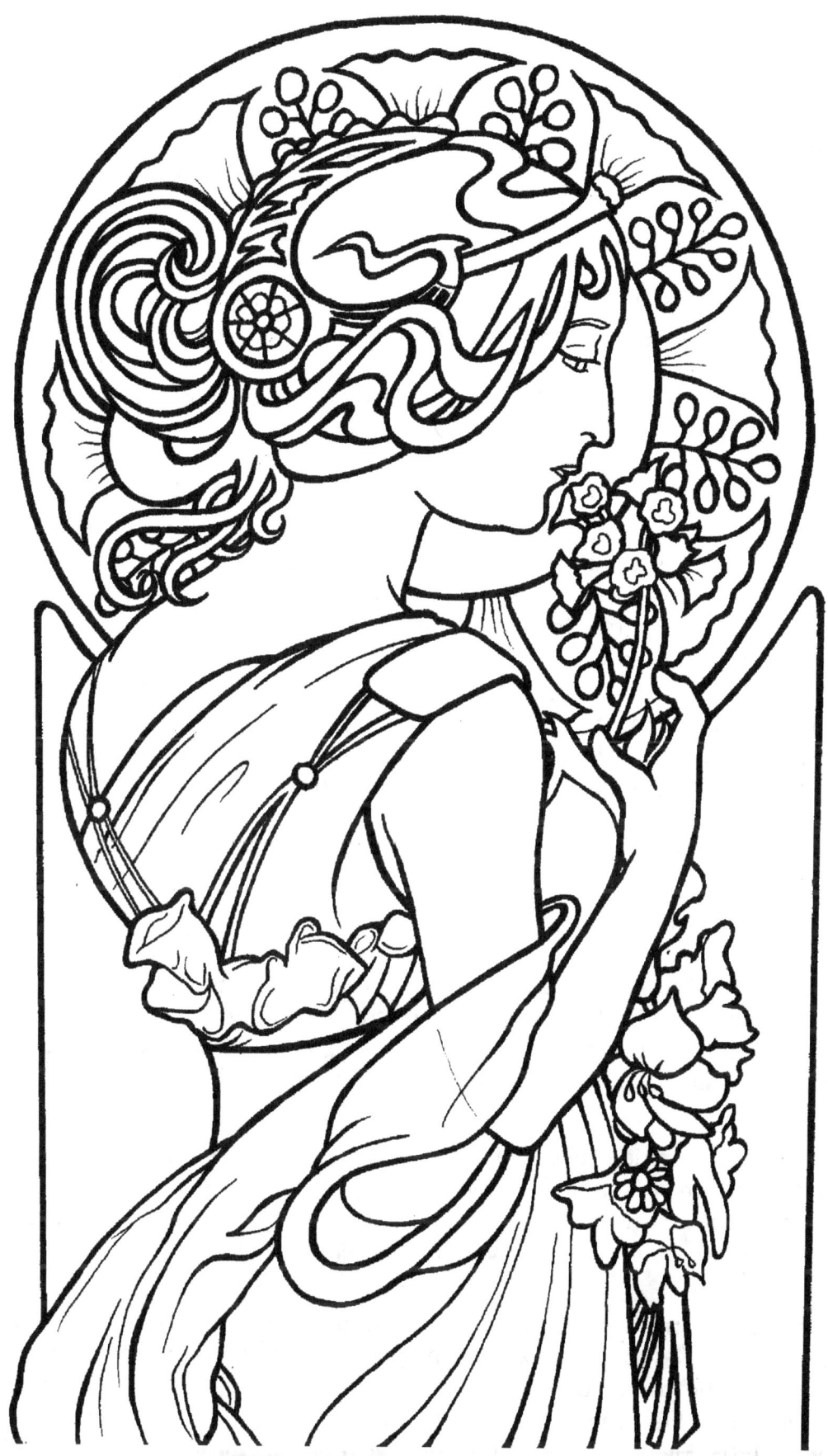

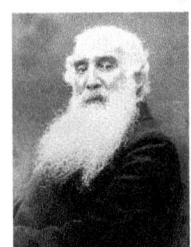

Camille Pissarro
(July 10, 1830 – November 13, 1903)

Jacob Abraham Camille Pissarro was born on the island of St. Thomas, in the Danish West Indies, on July 10, 1830. His parents were Frederick and Rachel Manzano de Pissarro; a marriage that caused quite a stir in their small Jewish community, since Rachel had previously been married to Frederick's uncle, a forbidden union per Jewish law. The couple had a total of four children between them.

At 12 years old, Pissarro was sent away to the Savary Academy in Passy, an area near Paris, France. During these years at the academy, he took an interest in art through the influence of Monsieur Savary himself, visiting the collections at the Louvre and exploring art with his own creations. By the age of 17, his passion for art was well established, and so, upon returning home, he pursued a career in art, rather than taking up the family business as his father had hoped he would.

Camille Pissarro was a very influential artist of the Impressionist movement, from its beginning and into the time of Post Impressionism. He was a key figure in the development of this art style; inspiring great painters such as, Gauguin, Cézanne, Seurat and van Gogh, among many other artists during his lifetime and into the future art world. Pissarro's style was a continual evolution and exploration, but one thing that did stay constant was his subject matter. He most enjoyed painting everyday scenes; street traffic, snowy landscapes, the countryside and its people etc.

Pissarro also studied at the Académie Suisse. While working at the Académie, he met both Claude Monet and Paul Cézanne, which led to him also meeting Alfred Sisley and Pierre-Auguste Renoir. These fellow artists would all greatly inspire one another and share in the progress and success of the Impressionism movement.

In 1871 Pissarro married Julie Vellay, his mother's maid. Together, the couple would have eight children, one of which died at birth. They resided just outside of Paris in Pontoise and then later in Louveciennes. Both places would inspire many of his landscape paintings, portraying the people of his village at work and at play.

Later in life, Pissarro had a continual eye infection that prevented him from painting outdoors, as he so loved to do. However, the passionate painter did not let this hindrance stop him. Instead, he continued to paint the outdoor scenes from the window view of various hotel rooms. He continued painting throughout his life, until he died in Paris on November 13, 1903. He was buried in the Père Lachaise Cemetery.

Chestnut Trees at Louveciennes (1872) By Camille Pissarro

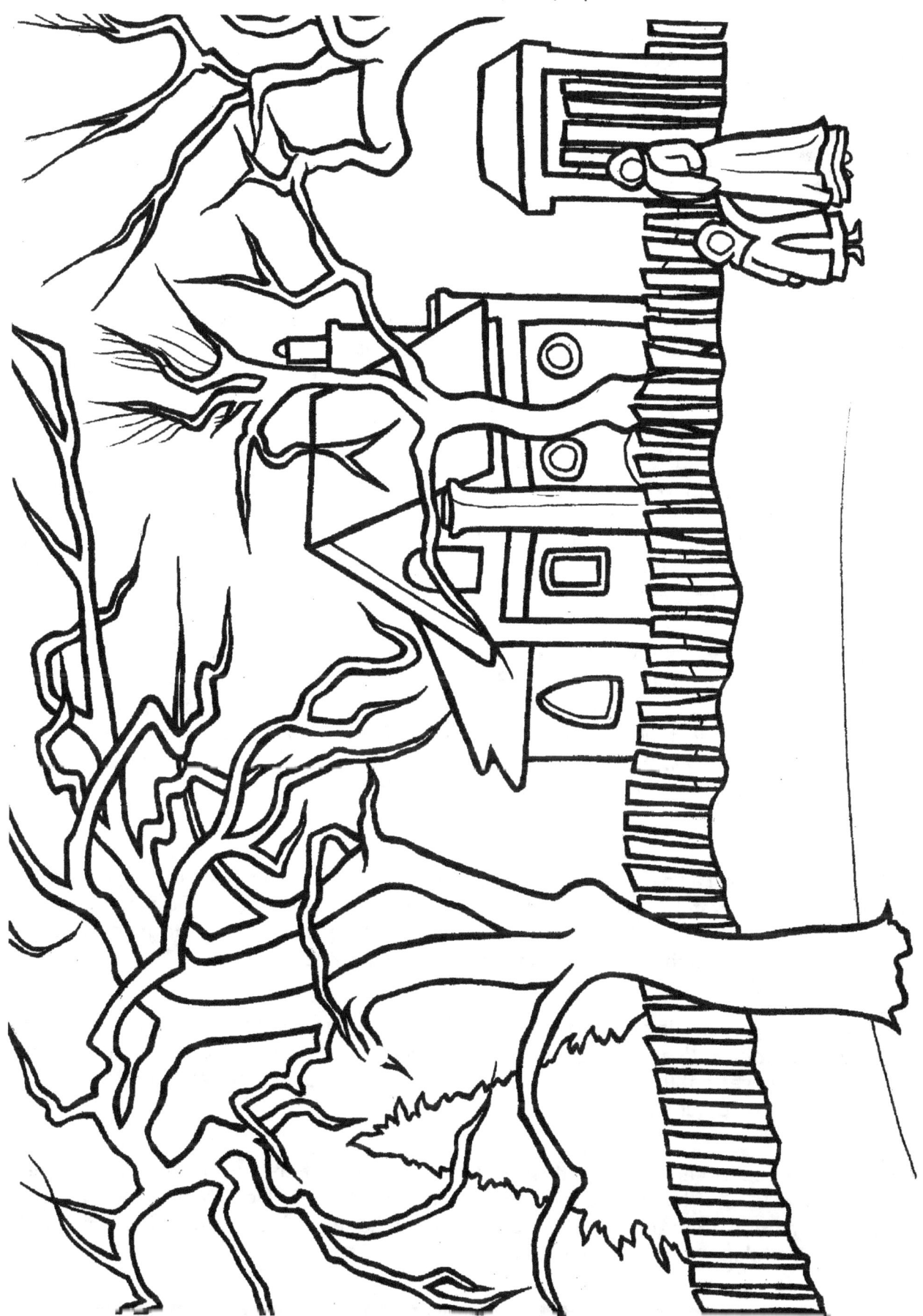

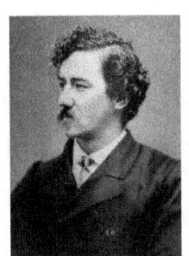

James Whistler
(July 10, 1834 – July 17, 1903)

🎨 James Abbott McNeill Whistler was born on July 10, 1834. He was born in Lowell, Massachusetts, although he later claimed his birthplace to be St. Petersburg, Russia. He was quoted, having said, "I shall be born when and where I want, and I do not choose to be born in Lowell."[1] Perhaps this is where he was born as an artist. He was the first child of George Washington Whistler and Anna Matilda McNeill.

🎨 Being a moody child, Whistler's parents quickly realized that drawing soothed his temper, calming and helping him to focus. He was given private art lessons for a time, later attending the Imperial Academy of Fine Arts at the age of 11. Encouraged by a fellow artist, his brother-in-law, Whistler attended lectures and art collections, deciding that his future career would most certainly be as an artist. In 1855 Whistler left for Paris, to further his studies in painting. He never returned to the United States, finally claiming London as his home.

🎨 James Whistler was an American artist who was known for his printmaking, writing and, most notably, for his monotone paintings. He had an unusual way of naming his paintings; using terms like "harmonies", "arrangements" and "nocturnes", as if the tones of the paintings were music. The painting that he is most famous for, "*Whistler's Mother*", was actually titled *Arrangement in Grey and Black No. 1*. Another popular work, "*The White Girl*", was titled *Symphony in White, No. 1*. His nighttime, moonlit paintings of the harbor and such, were called "Nocturnes".

🎨 Whistler also had a unique way of signing his paintings that had evolved over the years. His famous signature began by using his initials J.M.W. and was in the shape of a butterfly with a long stinger for its tail. The "J" formed the body and stinger tail, the "M" formed the upper arches of the wings and the "W" formed the lower arches of the wings.

🎨 On August 11, 1888 James Whistler was married to Beatrice Godwin, a former student. His painting, *Harmony in Red: Lamplight*, portrays his wife. Sadly, Beatrix died of cancer after only 8 years of marriage, in 1896. The couple never had children together, though Whistler did father several illegitimate children.

🎨 After the death of his wife, Whistler was devastated and withdrew from society. Seven years later, Whistler died of heart disease in London on July 17, 1903. He is buried at St. Nicholas Church in Chiswick, West London. Whistler's childhood home, at 243 Worthen Street in Lowell, is now the Whistler House Museum of Art.

Arrangement in Grey and Black No. 1 / Whistler's Mother (1871) by James Whistler

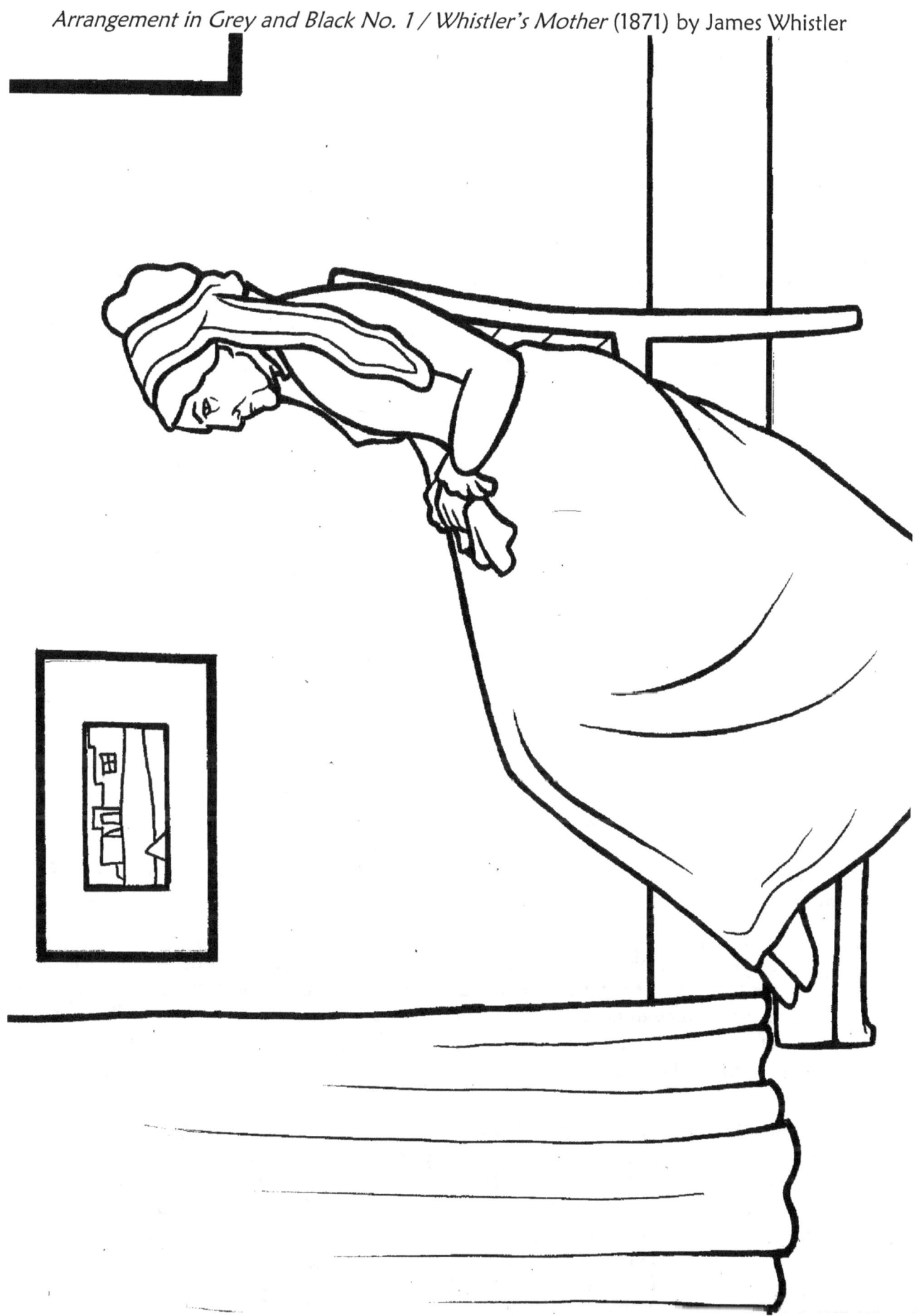

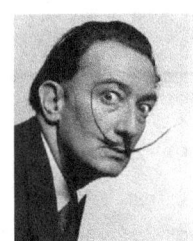

Salvador Dali
(May 11, 1904 – January 23, 1989)

Salvador Felipe Jacinto Dalí y Domenech was born on May 11, 1904, in Figueres, Catalonia, Spain. His mother, the greatest supporter of her son's artistic endeavors, was Felipa Domenech Ferrés, His father, Salvador Dalí y Cusí, was a lawyer and notary. Salvador had a sister, Anna Maria, and a brother who died in childhood.

Dali attended art school in 1916, where he focused on charcoal drawing. Only 3 years later, in 1919, he would have his first public exhibition. In 1922, the young artist decided to further his education and began studying at the Real Academia de Bellas Artes de San Fernando. In 1934 Dalí's art was introduced to the United States by art dealer, Julien Levy. The exhibition was held in New York, including his most memorable piece, *Persistence of Memory*. His work was an immediate sensation.

Dali's painting style began by exploring Cubism and Dadaism, after being influenced by artists such as Pablo Picasso, whom he had met during his visit to Paris in 1926. However, Dali eventually found his true passion in Surrealism-- painting the bizarre landscapes of his mind. He was best known for the unusual and often shocking content of his artwork, although, his eccentric behavior and personal style often commanded equal attention. Dali also worked in photography, film and sculpture.

Later in life, Dalí spoke of his brother who had passed away months before his own birth. This brother had also been named Salvador. Dalí often told the story of a time, when he was 5 years old, that his parents had taken him to the graveside of his brother and told him that he was his reincarnation. Dali once said that his brother "was probably a first version of myself, but conceived too much in the absolute."

In 1929, Dalí met his muse, Elena Ivanovna Diakonova (Gala), who was, at the time, married to the Surrealist writer, Paul Éluard. Gala found a deep connection with Dali and soon left her husband to be with him. The two were eventually married in 1934 by civil ceremony, and later remarried in a Catholic church in 1958. The couple had an unusual and open relationship, with no children.

In 1968, Dalí bought a castle in Púbol for his wife Gala. This castle became her private sanctuary, where Dali agreed not to visit without permission. In 1982, Gala died, sending Dali into a deep depression. He lost his will to live and to paint, announcing what would be his final painting, *The Swallows Tail*, in 1983. In November of 1988, Dalí was taken to the hospital for heart failure. On the morning of January 23, 1989, while his favorite record played, Dalí passed away at the age of 84. He is buried in the crypt below the stage of his Theatre and Museum in Figueres, across the street from the Church of Sant Pere, where he had been baptized, received his first communion and finally his funeral.

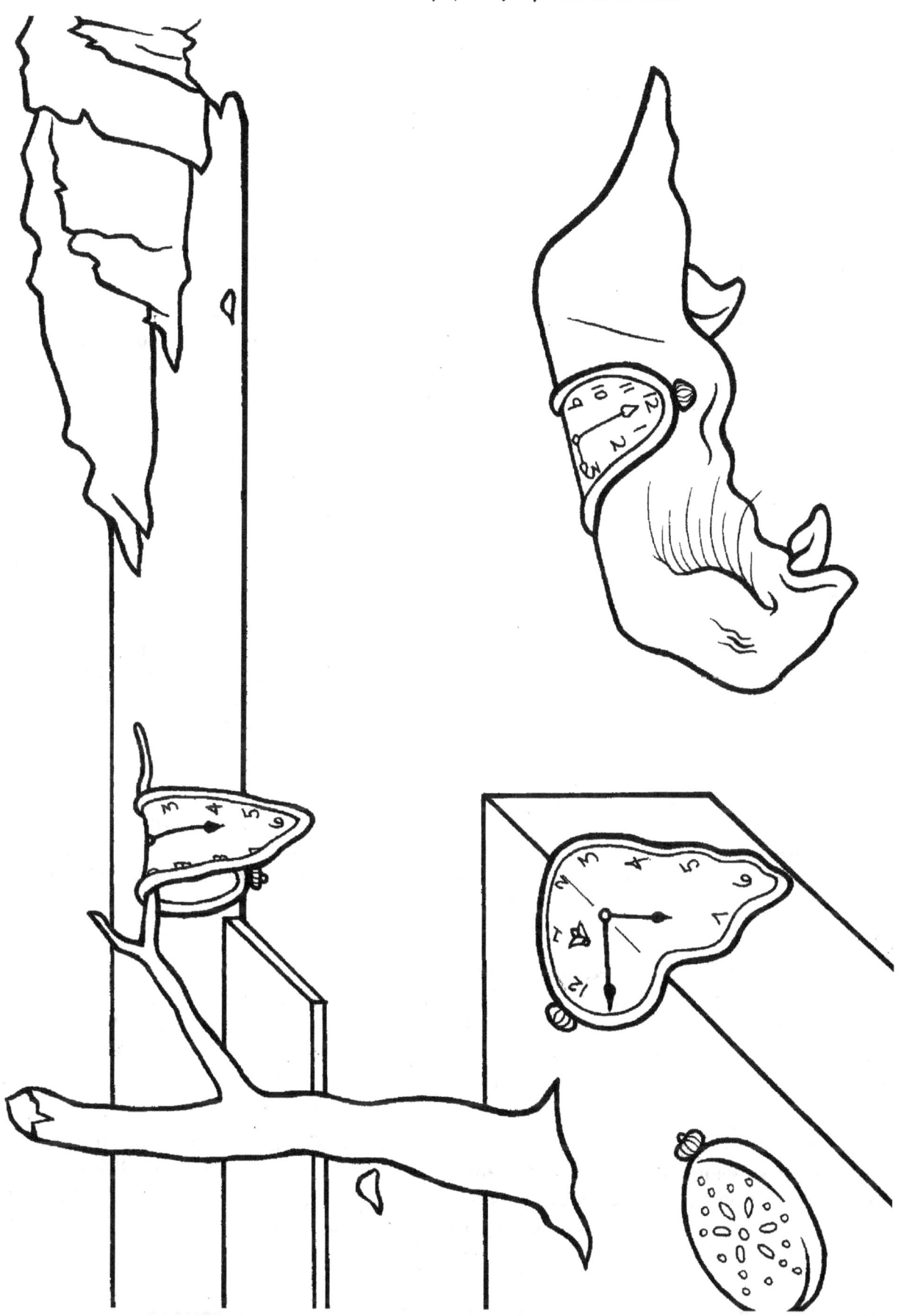

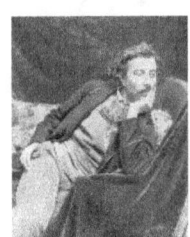

Paul Gauguin
(June 7, 1848 – May 8, 1903)

Eugène Henri Paul Gauguin was born on June 7, 1848 in Paris, France. His father, Clovis Gauguin, was a journalist; his mother, Alina Maria Chazal, was the daughter of an engraver. As a child, when Gauguin's father's employment ended with the newspaper, the family left France for Peru, however, Clovis died of a heart attack during their journey. Alina, now widowed with two small children, was welcomed by her granduncle, the father-in-law of the president of Peru. They would enjoy a privileged life for the next 6 years, until the family fell out of favor.

Gauguin's journey into art was different than our previous artists. He did not get an early start in his career; rather, he spent the early years of his life serving in the merchant marines and then with the French Navy. After the military, he became a stockbroker, where he began painting in his free time. During this period, he met and become friends with Camille Pissarro and Paul Cézanne, with whom he often painted. When the market fell, in 1883, Gauguin wrote to Pissarro that he would now paint full-time.

Gauguin enjoyed painting, but his art was not truly appreciated until after his death. In time, his paintings would become quite influential to many modern artists, such as Henri Matisse and Pablo Picasso. Gauguin's style is best-known for his experimental use of color, primitive form and style. Along with his love of painting, Gauguin was also a printmaker, sculptor and writer.

As Gauguin pursued a career in art, he met and became quick friends with Vincent van Gogh; although, this later proved to be a toxic relationship. In late 1888, the two friends had an argument, which led up to Van Gogh cutting off part of his own left ear, wrapping up the severed part and handing it to a woman, asking her to, "keep this object carefully, in remembrance of me."[1]

In 1873, Gauguin married Mette-Sophie Gad, a Danish woman. The couple lived in Copenhagen, Denmark, where they had five children: Émile (1874–1955), Aline (1877–1897), Clovis (1879–1900), Jean René (1881–1961) and Paul Rollon (1883–1961). The marriage deteriorated after about 11 years when Gauguin's business began to fail. The couple separated in 1885, finally ending the relationship around 1894.

Gauguin longed to escape European society, and so, in 1891 he fled to Tahiti. However, He was quite disappointed to discover that Tahiti had been much westernized. In 1901, he moved once more, this time to the Marquesas Islands. Gauguin was financially destitute, with his health declining after several heart attacks and advancing syphilis. On May 8, 1903, Gauguin died alone in his island home. He is buried in the Atuona Cemetery.

Redheaded Woman and Sunflowers (1890) By Paul Gauguin

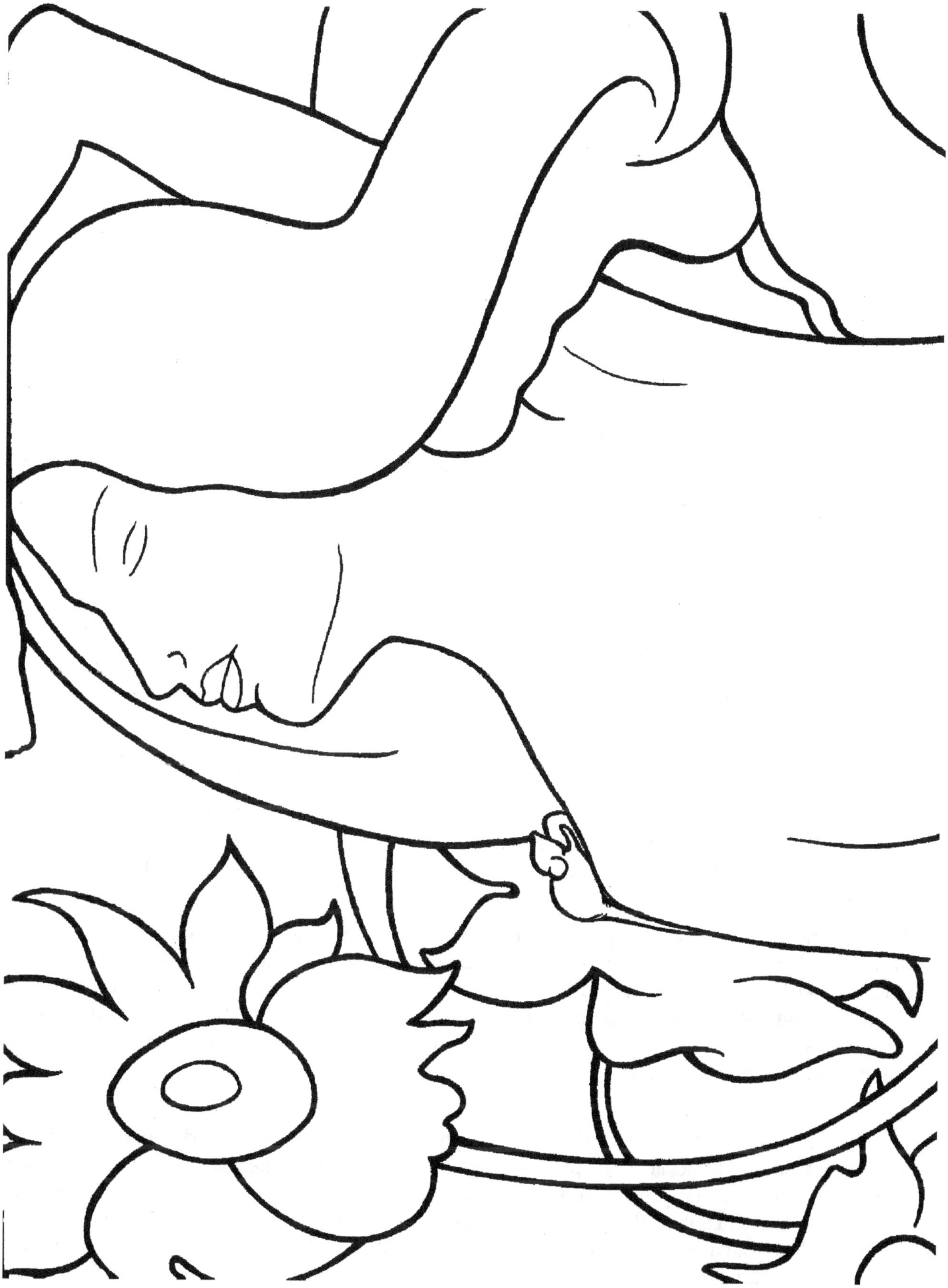

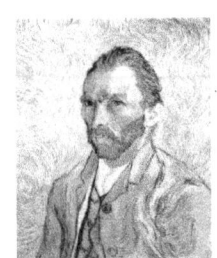

Vincent van Gogh
(March 30, 1853 – July 29, 1890)

Vincent Willem van Gogh was born on March 30, 1853 in Zundert, Netherlands. His parents were Theodorus van Gogh and Anna Cornelia Carbentus. Vincent was named for his grandfather and for his brother who had been stillborn a year before his own birth. He had two brothers; Theo and Cor, and three sisters: Elisabeth, Anna and Wilhelmina. Vincent only stayed close with Theo and Wilhelmina.

Vincent's education began with his mother, who encouraged his passion for art. In 1860 he was sent to the village school, followed by boarding school. This separation from his family was hard and he felt abandoned, continually pleading to come home; he was denied and instead, sent to another school in Tilburg. Here, he would have formal lessons in art, although he was still miserable and feeling abandoned.

For most modern-day artists, the word *Impressionism* instantly brings Vincent van Gogh to mind, as he was one of the most influential painters of that movement. However, even though he is much-loved today, van Gogh only sold one painting in his lifetime. His work was not popular during his career, even with his brother being an art dealer. Ultimately, Vincent thought himself to be an utter failure as an artist.

Vincent's early work was more subdued in color and subject, Theo said it was "too dark". His later work, however, is characterized by bold, vibrant colors and dramatic brushwork-- scenes coming alive with the flow of emotion evident in every brush stroke. Van Gogh painted still-life, landscapes, portraits and self-portraits.

Vincent never married and had no known children. He did live with a woman, Clasina Maria "Sien" Hoornik, but his father disapproved and he eventually left her in 1883. Sien drowned herself in the River Scheldt in 1904. In 1884 Vincent began a relationship with Margot Begemann, his neighbour's daughter. The couple would have married, but their families protested, after which Margot overdosed herself with strychnine. She was saved by Van Gogh, who rushed her to the hospital.

Vincent consistently neglected his health; living on bread, coffee and tobacco, drinking heavily of absinthe. In addition to poor physical health, Vincent's mental health had also been in question; an issue that came painfully to light when Gauguin came to see him in 1888. The visit ended with Vincent cutting off part of his own ear during an argument. Two years later, Vincent walked out into a field and shot himself in the chest. He did not die instantly and managed to walk back to his apartment. Theo rushed to his brother's side as he spoke his final words, "The sadness will last forever". He died 2 days later, on July 29, 1890, and was buried in the municipal cemetery of Auvers-sur-Oise.

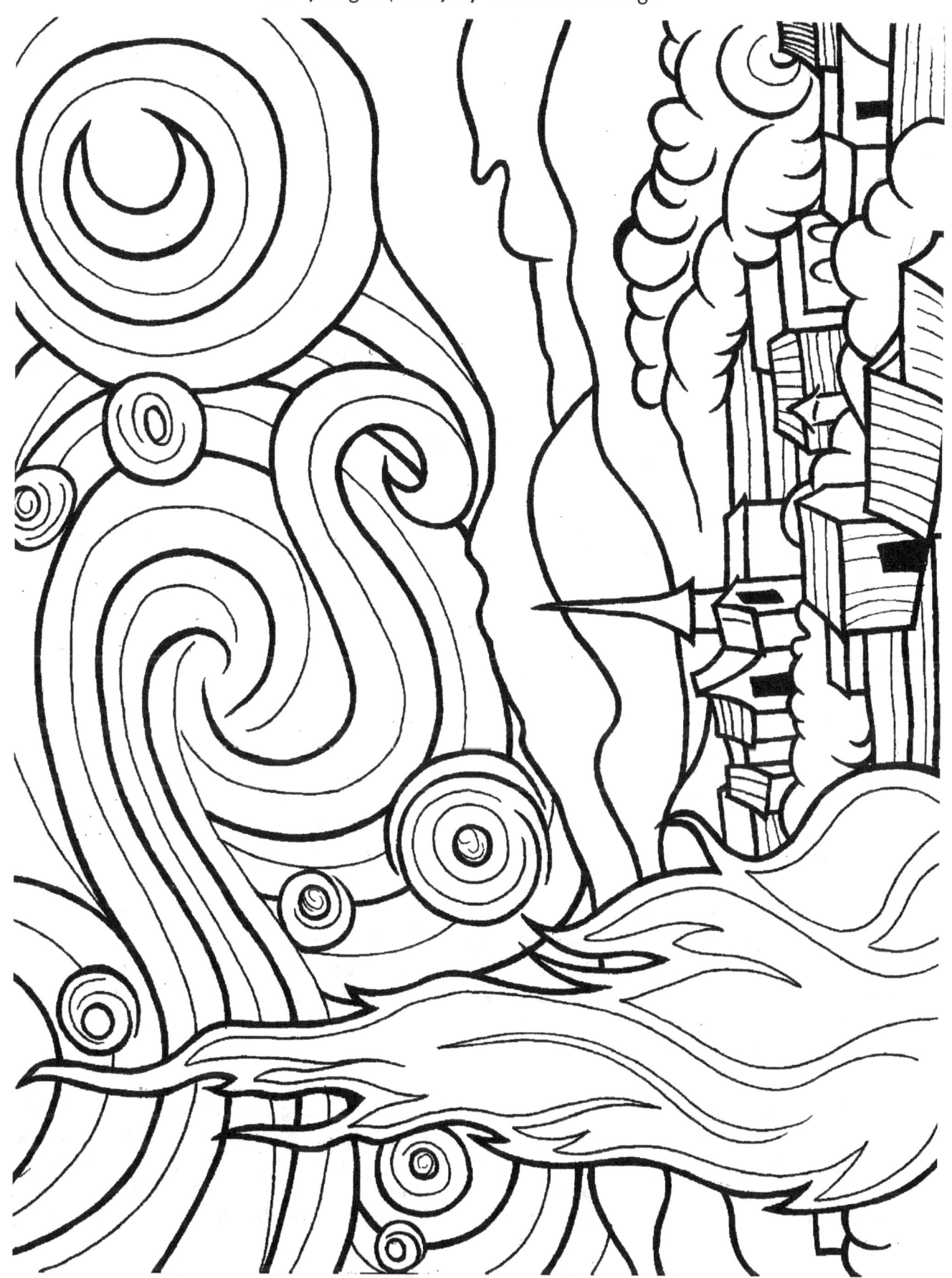

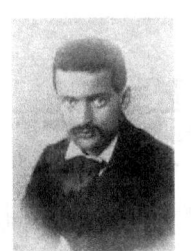

Paul Cezanne
(January 19, 1839 – October 22, 1906)

Paul Cezanne was born on January 19, 1839 in the Aix-en-Provence of France. His parents were Louis-Auguste Cézanne and Anne Elisabeth Honorine Aubert. He had two younger sisters.

In 1858, Cezanne followed in his father's wishes and attended law school at the *University of Aix-en*. However, much to his father's dismay, Cezanne had no taste for law and chose not to continue in his legal education. Instead, he left for Paris in 1861, to pursue a career in art. His father was quite upset with his choice, but the two eventually made peace and he supported his son's artistic career. Upon his father's death, Cezanne found that his father had left him a large inheritance of $400,000, giving him the freedom to continue pursuing his passion in art.

In Paris, Cezanne met and became friends with the Impressionist artist, Camille Pissaro. He admired Pissaro's work and began studying alongside him as they often painted landscapes together *en plein-air*. Cézanne's early work was very imaginative, whereas his later work reflects the time that he spent with Pissarro, working from actual observation instead. His work is distinguished by repetitive, small brushstrokes that accumulate to form the completed image in his own style of *Impressionism*.

Cezanne was another great artist whose work was first exhibited in the *Salon des Refusés;* a display for the work of artists that had been rejected by the official *Paris Salon.* He had been the figure of ridicule and insult in a derogatory article titled, "Love for the ugly". His art was not appreciated by the public at first, but Cezanne was regarded as a master by the art students who worked with him and later by great artists such as Picasso, Edgar Degas, Pierre-Auguste Renoir, Paul Gauguin and Henri Matisse. Cezanne continued to submit work to the Salon-- he eventually had one piece admitted; *Portrait de M. L. A.*

In 1886, Cezanne married Hortense Fiquet, a model that he had been living with for 17 years. The relationship was tumultuous and ended with Cezanne giving his wife and their son the estate of his father, while purchasing a piece of land for himself. He built a studio on the land and turned his attention to painting. Here, in this sanctuary, he would paint and live in isolation until the day of his death.

While painting outside one day, Cézanne was caught in a rainstorm. He continued working in the rain for a couple of hours before going home, collapsing on the way back. He died a few days later, on October 22, 1906 of pneumonia and/or diabetic complications. He is buried at the *Saint-Pierre Cemetery* in his hometown of Aix-en-Provence, France. By the time of his death, Cezanne had acquired the long-desired respect and status of a legendary figure in the art society.

Still life with apples 4 (c. 1893-94) By Paul Cezanne

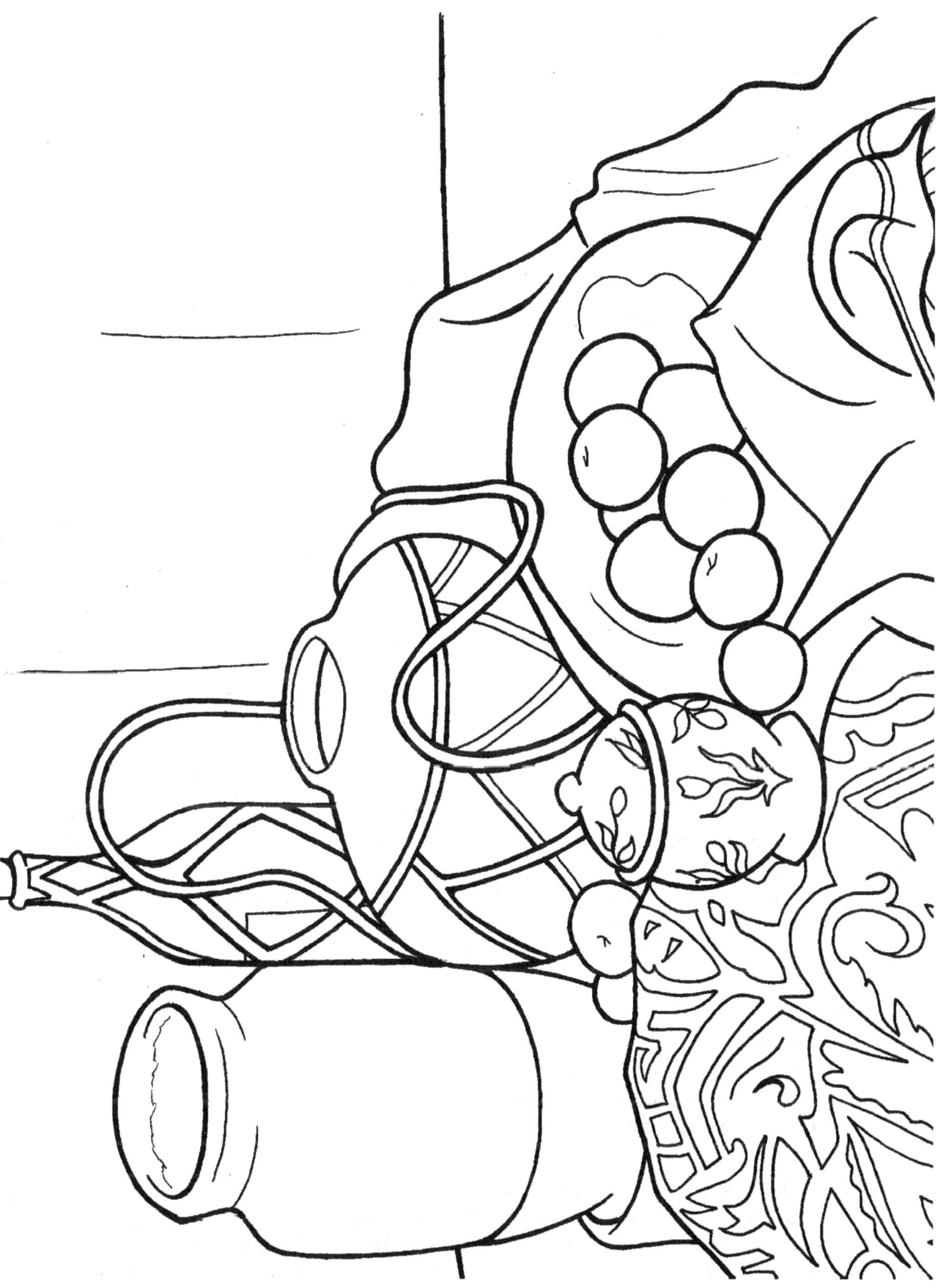

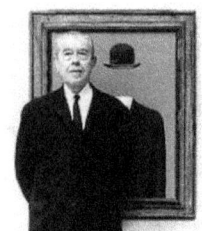

Rene Magritte
(November 21, 1898 – August 15, 1967)

René François Ghislain Magritte was born on November 21, 1898, in Lessines, Belgium. His father, Léopold Magritte, was a tailor; and his mother, Régina (née Bertinchamps), was a hat maker. He had two brothers, Paul and Raymond.

Magritte began drawing lessons in 1910 and did his first paintings in 1915, at the age of 17. In 1916 he attended the *Académie Royale des Beaux-Arts* in Brussels, studying with the Belgian muralist and sculptor, Constant Montald. He continued these studies for only two years, quitting the school in 1918, as he was feeling under-inspired and wanting to paint on his own. In December of 1920 Magritte served nearly one year in the Belgian infantry and then worked in a wallpaper factory until 1923, and as a poster ad designer until 1926. When he was finally contracted by the *Galerie 'Le Centaure'*, in Brussels, he began painting full-time. He first exhibition was in 1927.

Magritte is well known for the thought-provoking concepts and unusual use of subjects in his paintings, such as a business suit and hat on an invisible man, a man with a smoking pipe for a nose or lovers kissing with cloth covered faces. The young artist explored many styles of art throughout his career; his first paintings being very impressionistic in style, while later works drew inspiration from Cubism and Futurism, and still later, settling on his own style of Surrealism.

Magritte's mother had repeatedly tried to commit suicide, forcing her husband to lock her in her room. One day she managed to escape and was missing for 2 days, having finally managed drown herself in the River Sambre on March 12, 1912. Magritte would have been 13 years of age at the time and was rumored to have been there when her body was discovered, though this story was later discredited. The story was that, when her body was found, her dress had gone up to cover her face and that this possibly inspired much of Magritte's later work where he often covered the faces in cloth.

In 1922, Magritte married Georgette Berger. The two had first met when they were only 13, meeting again in 1920. Georgette quickly became Magritte's favorite model for a time. In 1936 Magritte damaged their marriage with an affair, and Georgette in turn had her own affair. The two did not reconcile for many years.

After a long and very hard struggle, Magritte succumbed to pancreatic cancer on August 15, 1967, at the age of 68. He was interred in *Schaerbeek Cemetery*, Evere, Brussels. You can visit Magritte's former home, which is now a museum, at 135 Rue Esseghem, in Brussels. There is a larger museum at the Place Royale in Brussels, that is dedicated to Magritte and has over 200 of his paintings, sculpture and drawings.

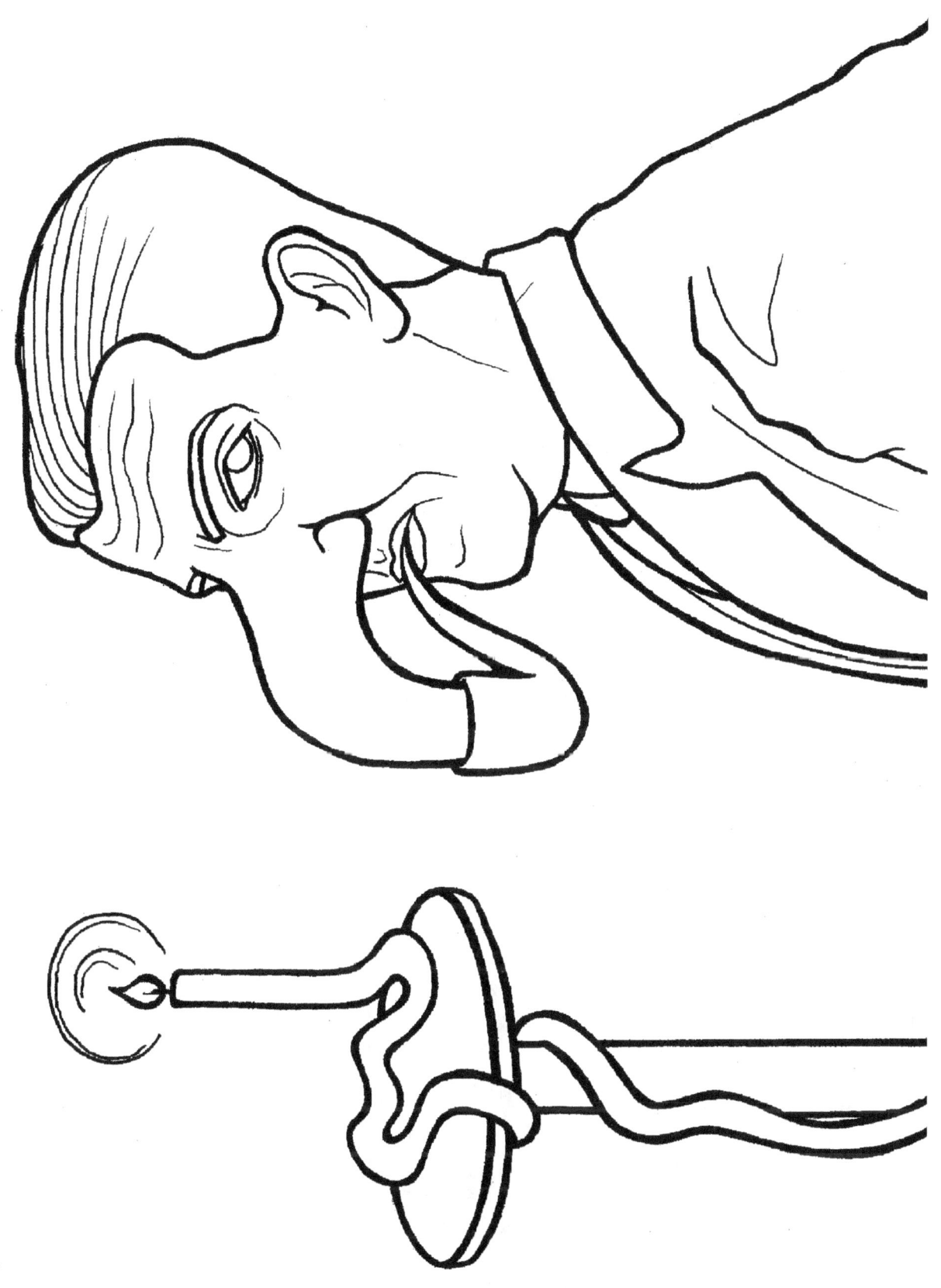

Keep up to date on Davina's latest publications, events,

contests and news by adding us on Facebook!

www.Facebook.com/DavinaRush

Also, visit DavinaRush.Com

About the Author

Davina Rush
(July 17, 1978)

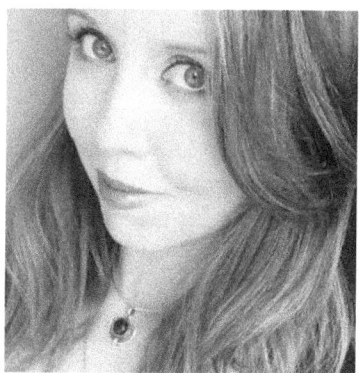

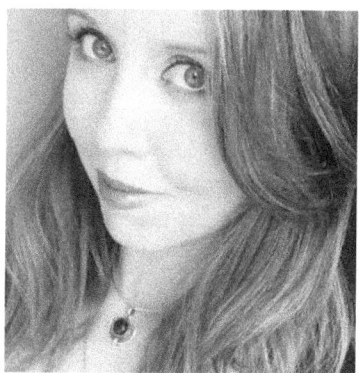 Davina Rush was born on July 17, 1978 in Northwest Florida. She has lived in Florida for most her life, but has also lived in Chattanooga, Tennessee and Springfield, Massachusetts; each for a few years. Her mother, father and two siblings all reside in Florida as well.

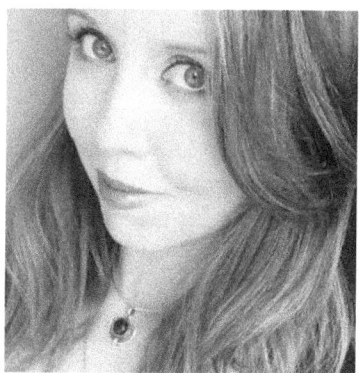 Davina's love for art began at an early age, before she even stepped foot into a school. Her first formal lessons, however, would not begin until she was around 12 years old and for a total of about 5 years, throughout middle school and a portion of high school. She furthered this education with an additional two years of instruction at the Chattanooga State College, where she focused on sculpting, drawing and oil painting. She has since continued her practice and her studies independently.

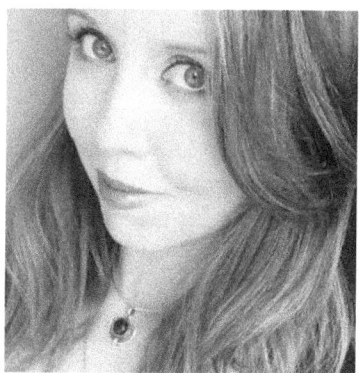 Davina's art has greatly evolved over the years. During her childhood and teen years, her artistic focus had been primarily on pencil and ink illustrations. As an adult, and after the very illuminating instruction during her years at college, she has now expanded her interest to include oil painting as her favored medium. In addition to these creative outlets, Davina also enjoys sculpting, assemblage, sewing and novel writing.

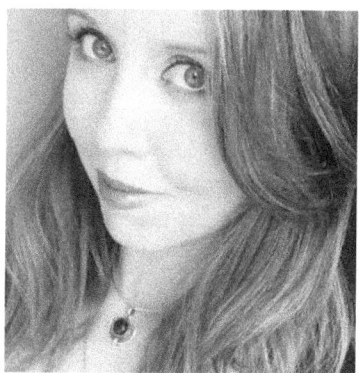 Davina's biggest influence in art, as far back as she can remember, has been the artist Tim Burton. Much of her earlier art reflects this admiration, though her more recent work is quite varied. Other artists that she greatly admires have included Vincent van Gogh, Frida Khalo, Lori Earley and Mark Ryden; as you might notice, these are all artists that paint with the dark and yet beautiful undertones of varied emotion.

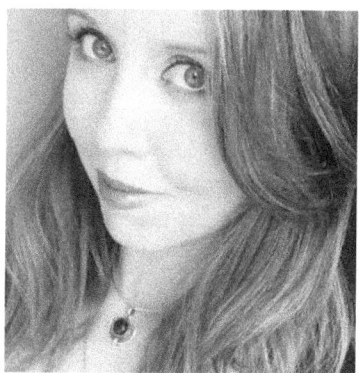 Davina's inspiration for her coloring books originally came from her daughters, in 2010. While drawing a picture of *Medusa* after writing a report on Greek Mythology for one of her classes, her daughters saw the illustration and asked if it was a "coloring page" and could they have one to color. At this very moment, as she handed over the "coloring page" to her daughters, the creative wheels began to turn and an idea was born. She would illustrate coloring books! Created for both children and adults, she would combine art with educational information—as she so greatly values learning. Her coloring books would be characterized by the combination of hand-drawn, boldly lined artwork and with the unusual choice of content, paired with educational information. Though she still has a great passion for painting—the illustration and writing of these coloring books have become her main career concentration,

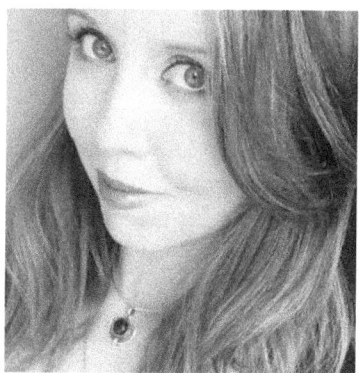 Davina now lives in the coastal city of Fort Walton Beach, Florida with her two daughters. She currently runs a small local business, while also pursuing her career as an artist and writer. Visit DavinaRush.com for more information.

Note from the Author

I hope you have enjoyed your coloring and learning experience with the *Famous Painters in Art History* as much as I have enjoyed creating this publication for you.

I have always loved art and admired the great artists that had the God-given talent for capturing what they saw and felt with the stroke of a pen or paintbrush. I enjoy learning all that I can about these great masters; their lives, their trials and triumphs, their inspirations and techniques and the legacies that they have left behind—made truly immortal through their collection of artwork. The inspiration for this book comes from that deep appreciation for art, but also from my Grandma who recently and playfully asked me, "Why are all of your books so creepy?", referring to my monster books. To this I answered, "I just love creepy stuff, Grandma", and then I wrote this book just for her. It has been a very educational and interesting journey and I truly hope you will enjoy my efforts.

Your purchase, comments, questions and reviews are greatly and sincerely appreciated. You can leave reviews on the website in which you purchased this book; and you can also write to me personally by joining my page at Facebook.com/DavinaRush. Get more information about me, as well as updates on my latest publications, events, contests and more by visiting my official website at www.DavinaRush.com

References

1. www.Wikipedia.com

2. www.Biography.com

3. grantwoodartgallery.org

4. johannes-vermeer.org

5. katsushikahokusai.org

6. pablopicasso.org

7. sandrobotticelli.org

8. modigliani.org

9. manet.org

10. titian.org

11. fridakahlo.org

12. georgesseurat.org

13. edvardmunch.org

14. leonardoda-vinci.org

15. gustavklimtart.org

16. albrecht-durer.org

17. okeeffemuseum.org

18. henrimatisse.org

19. pierre-auguste-renoir.org

20. edgar-degas.org

21. diegorivera.org

22. franciscogoya.org

23. caravaggio.org

24. michelangelo.org

25. claudemonet.org

26. rembrandtonline.org

27. alfonsmucha.org

28. camille pissarro.org

29. jamesabbottmcneillwhistler.org

30. salvador-dali.org

31. gauguin.org

32. vincent-van-gogh-gallery.org

33. paul-cezanne.org

34. renemagritte.org

35. Artic.edu/aic/collections/exhibitions/Munch/resource/171

36. Msu.edu/course/ha/446/panter.htm